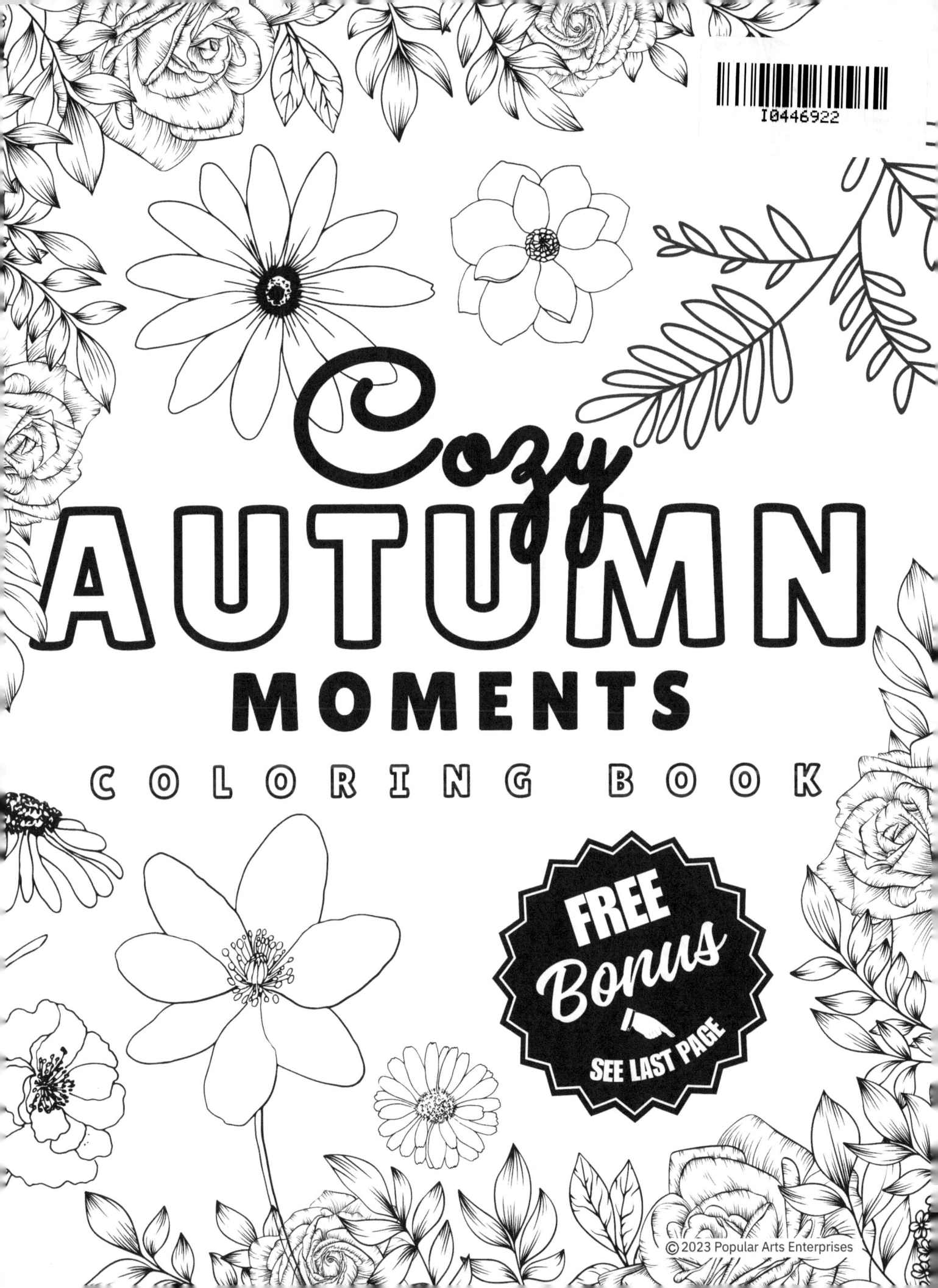

Cozy AUTUMN MOMENTS
COLORING BOOK

FREE Bonus
SEE LAST PAGE

I0446922

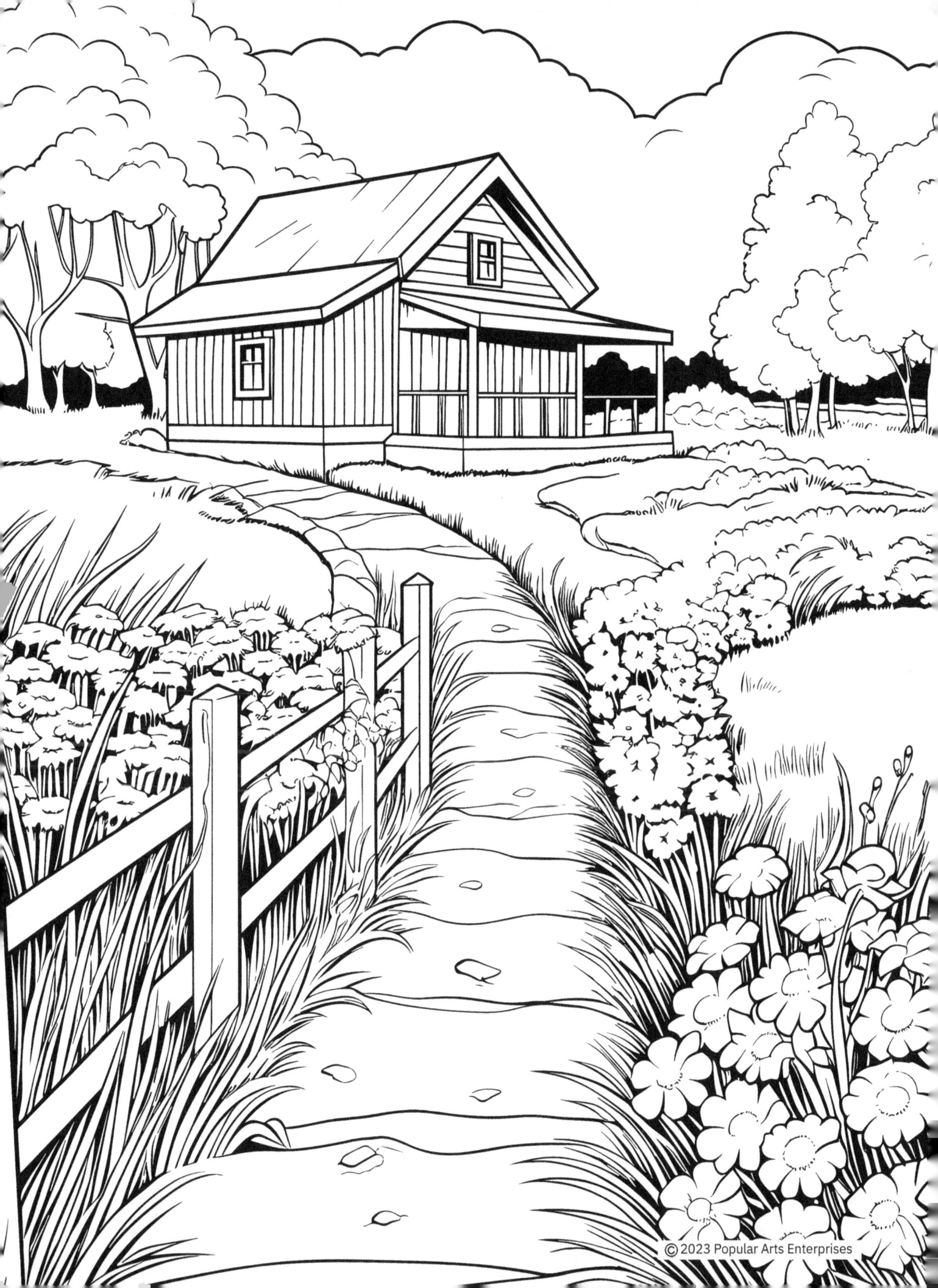

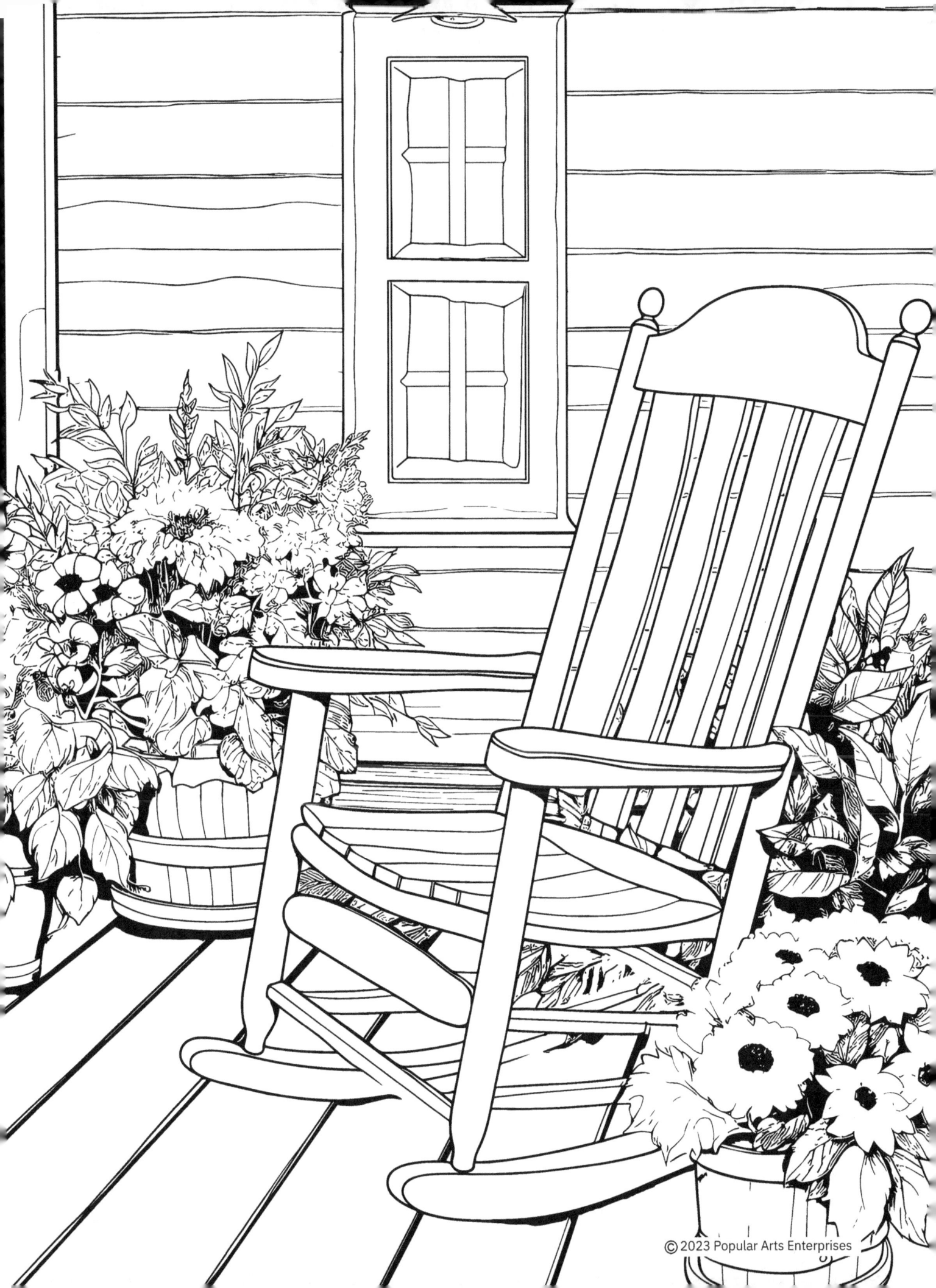

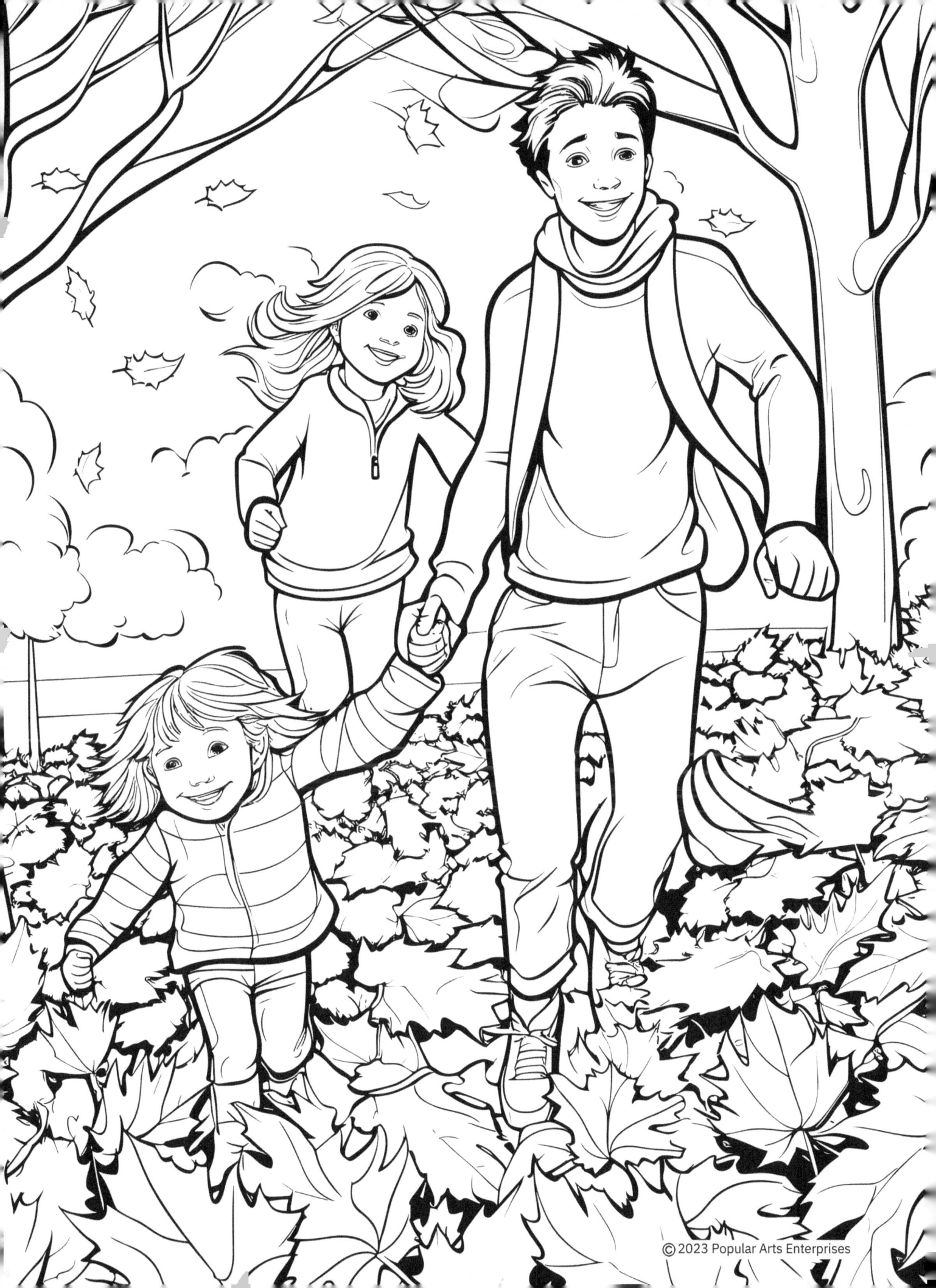

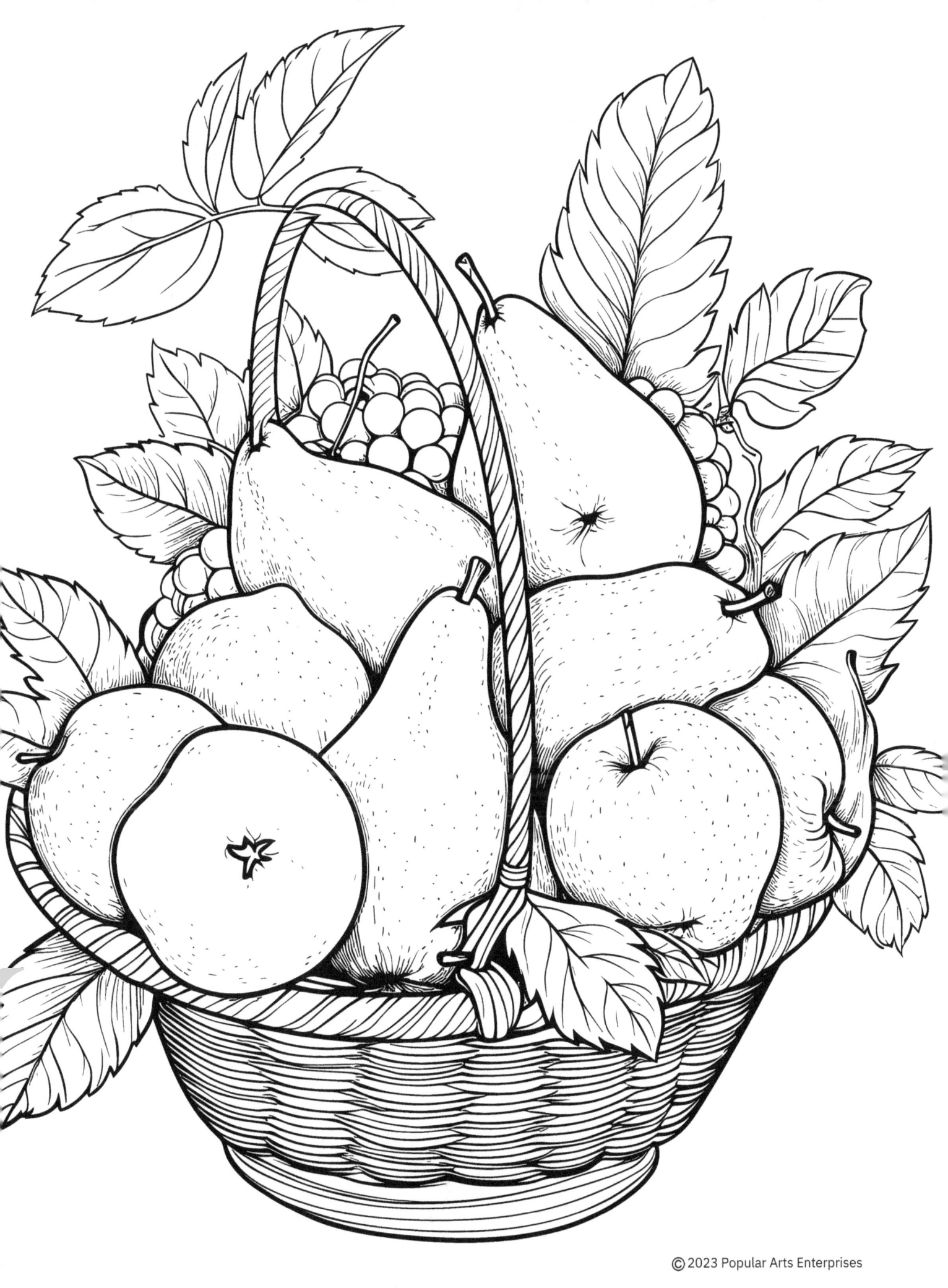

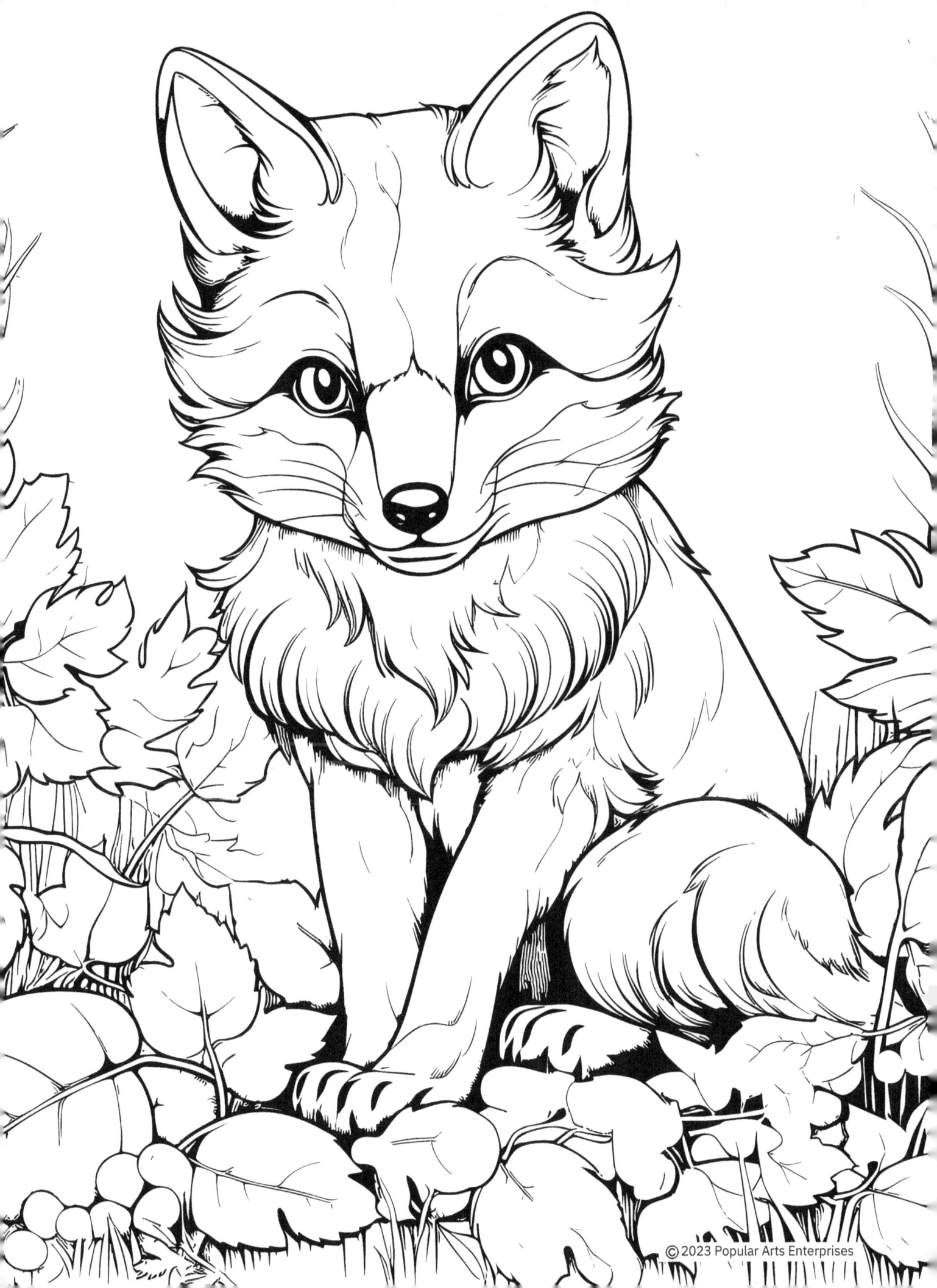

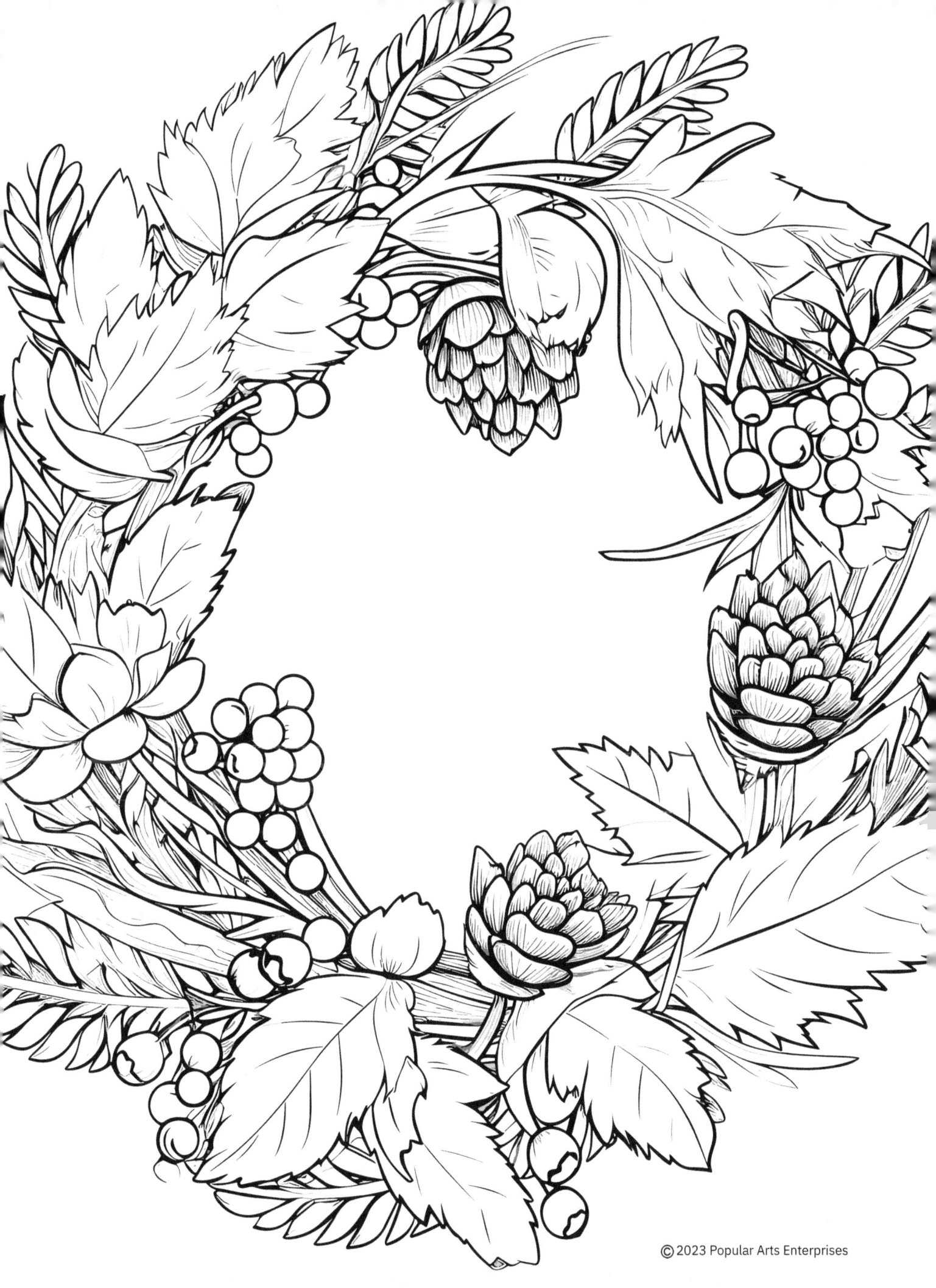

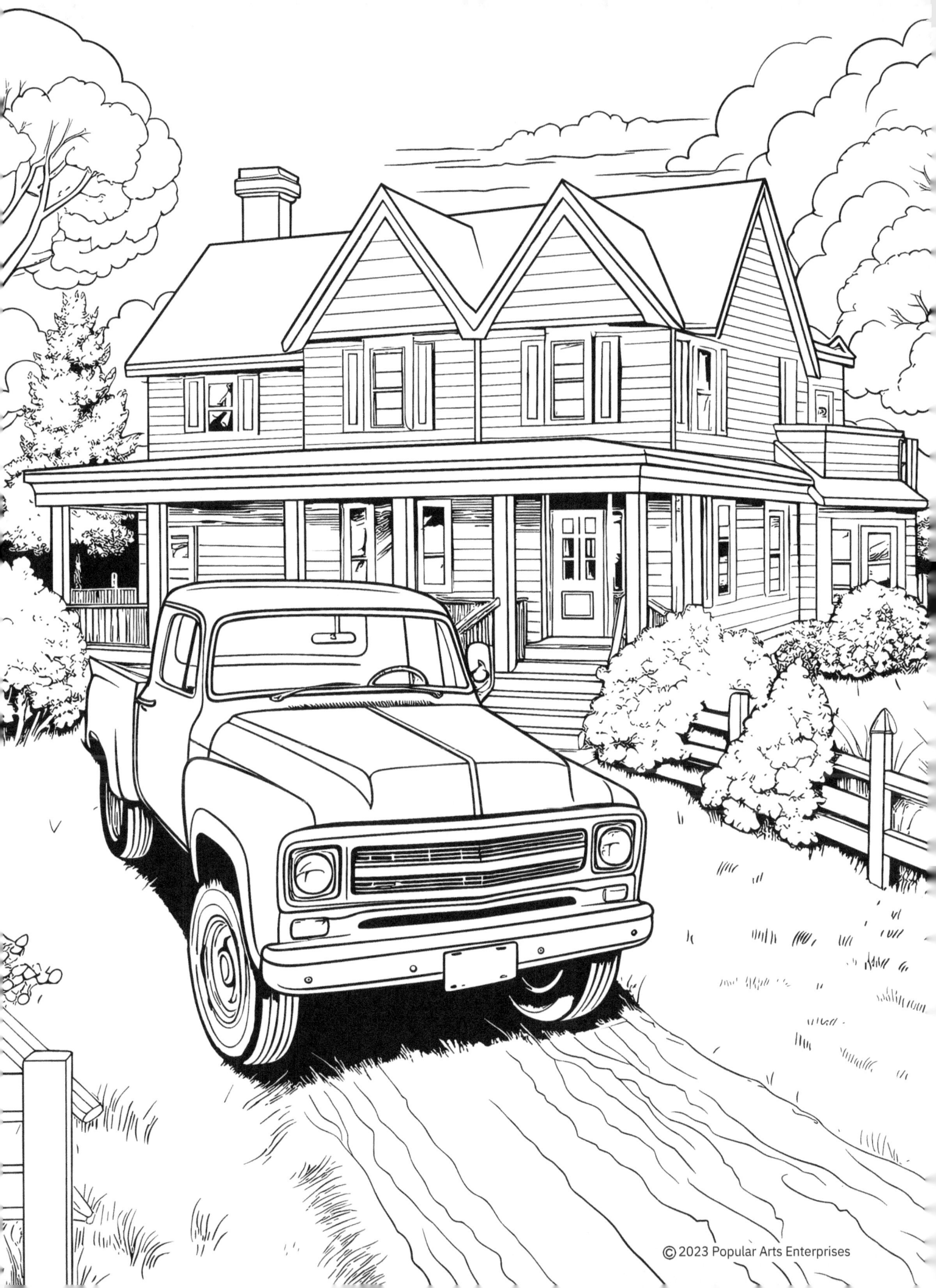

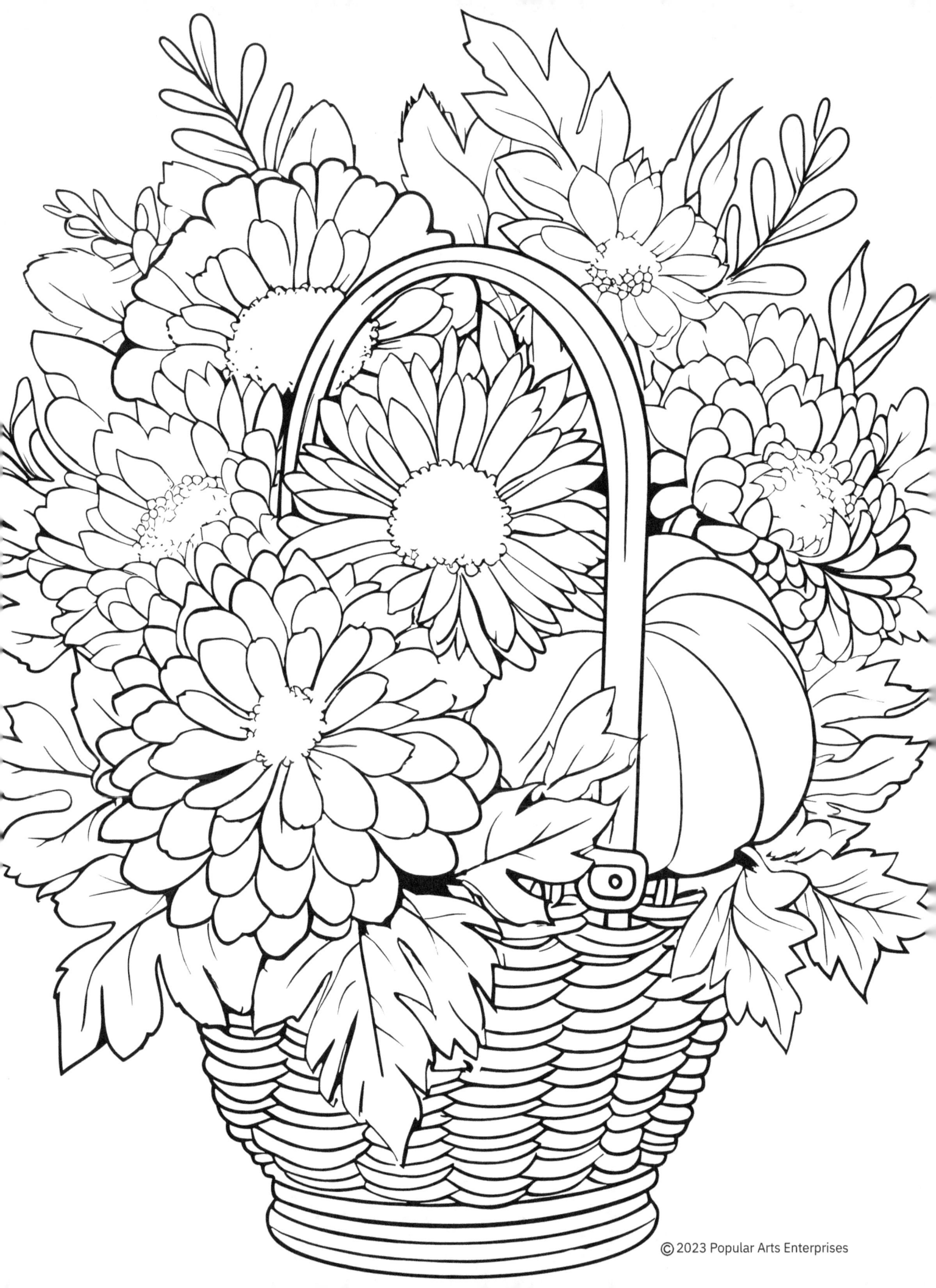

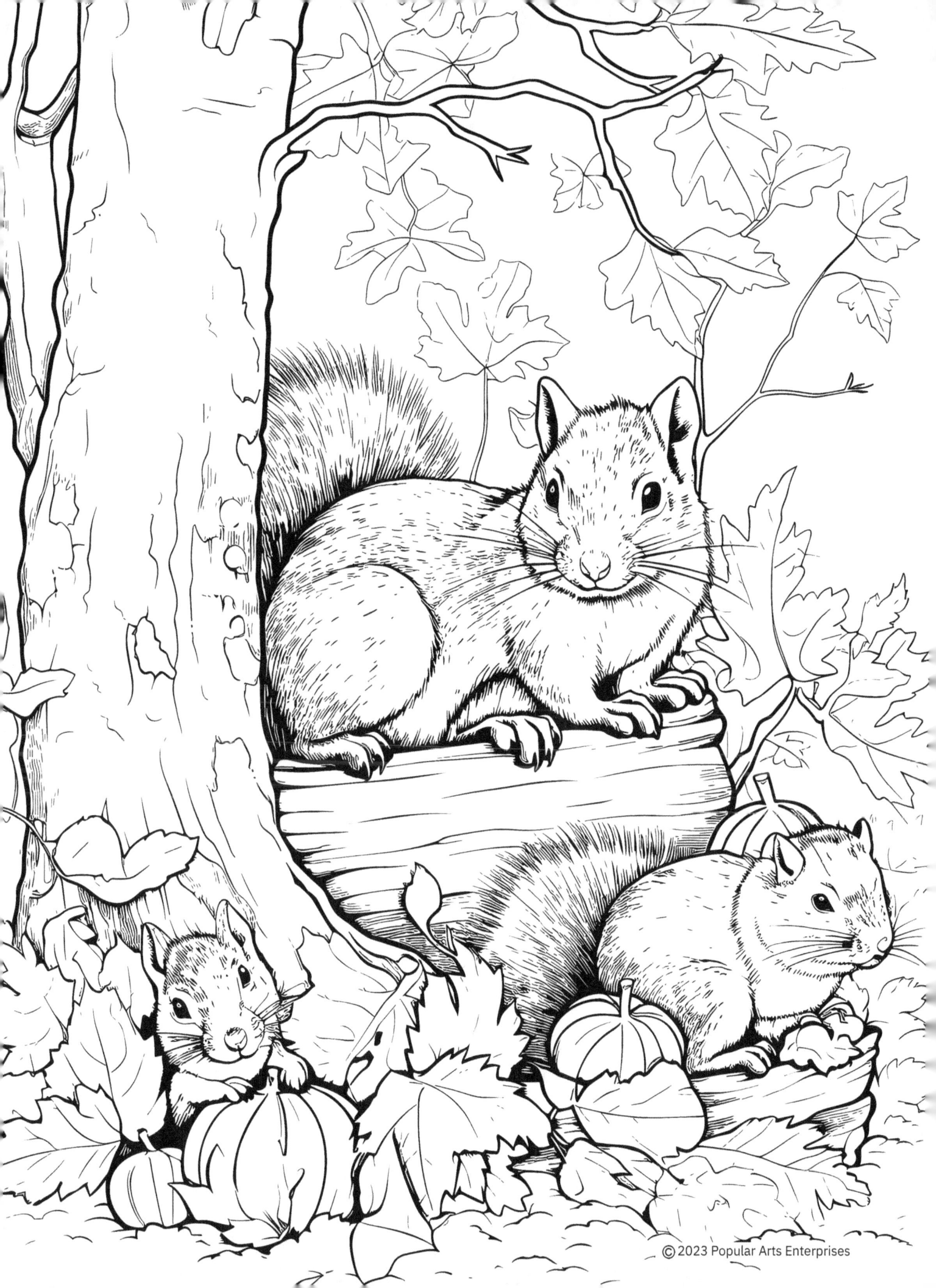

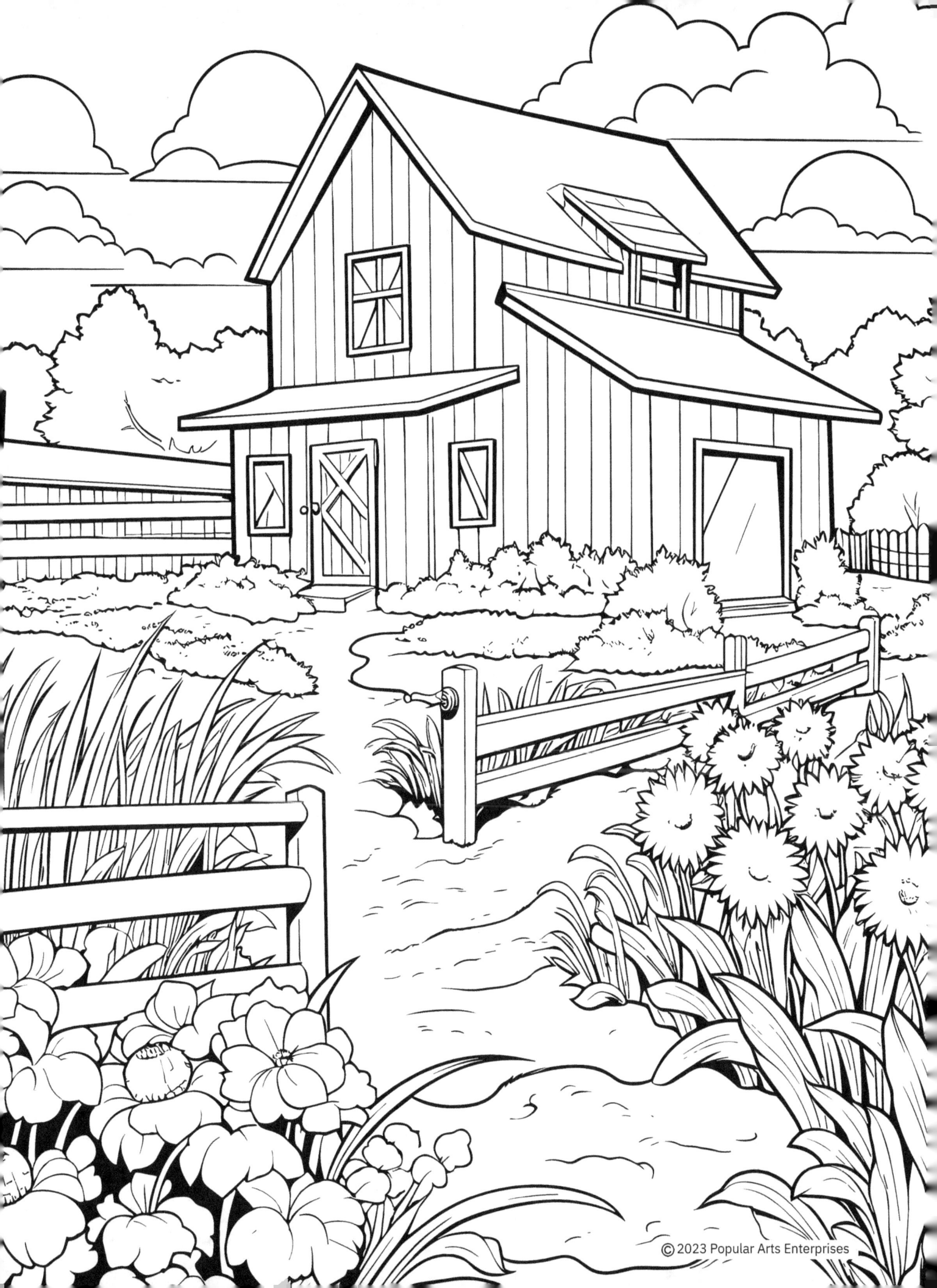

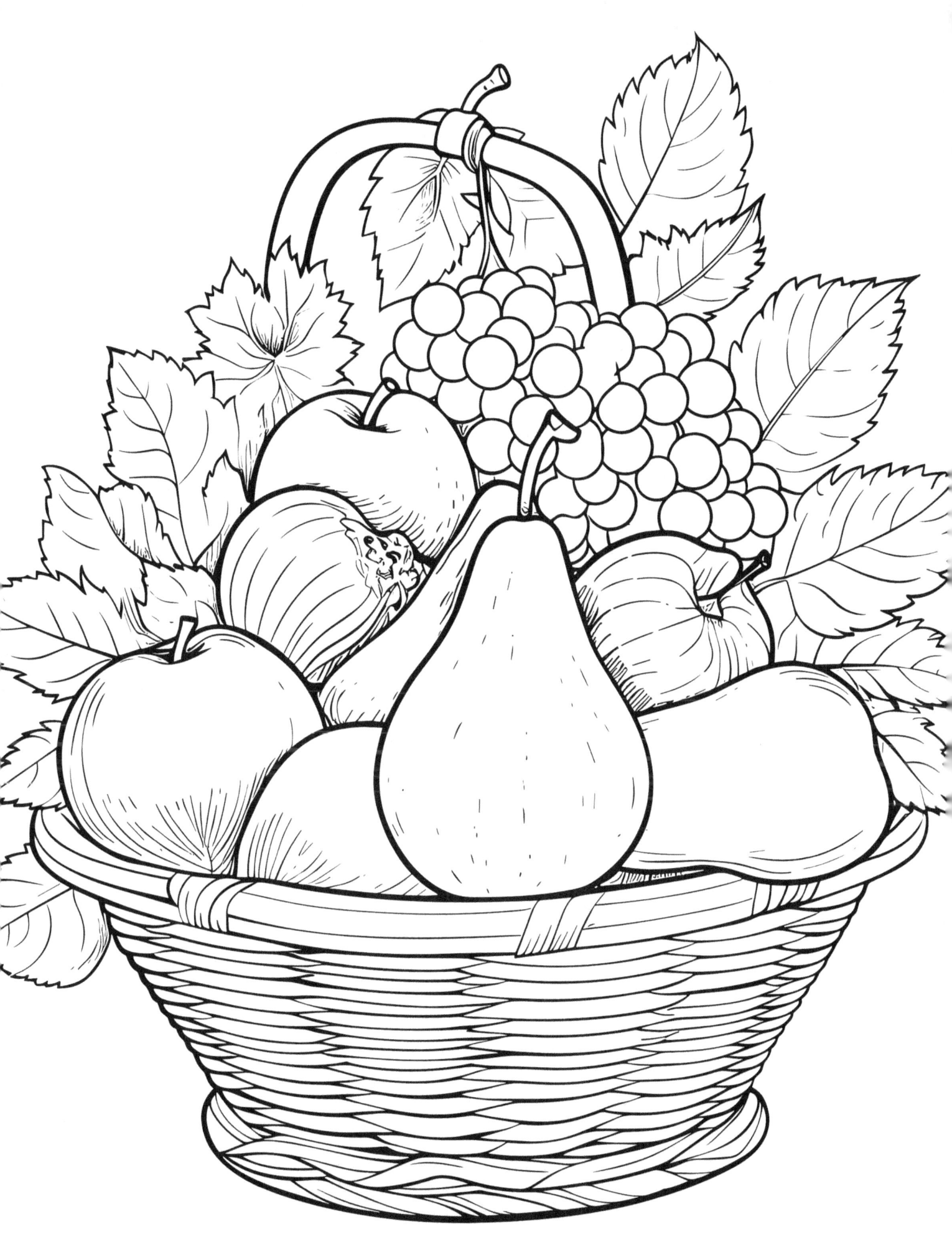

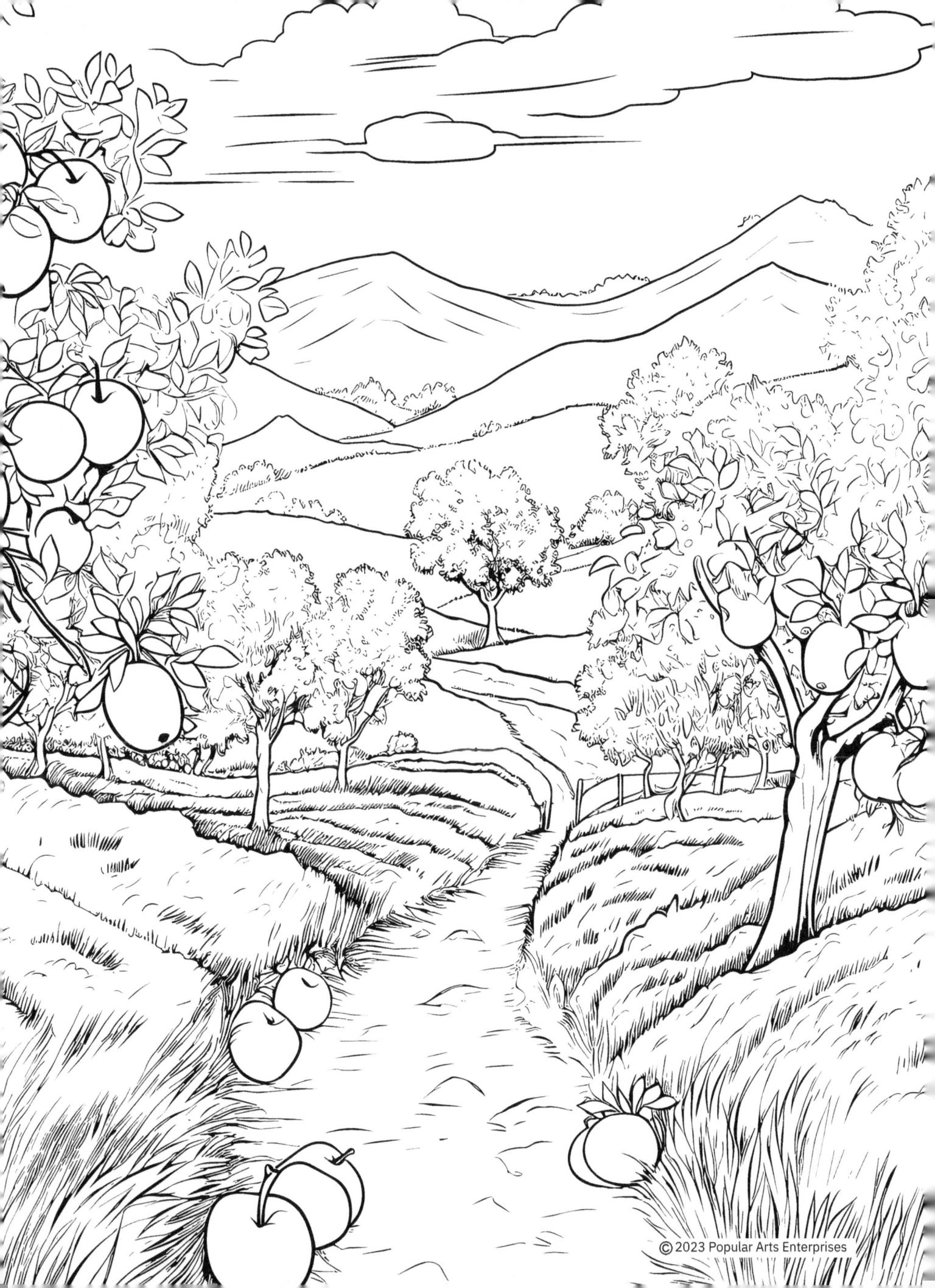

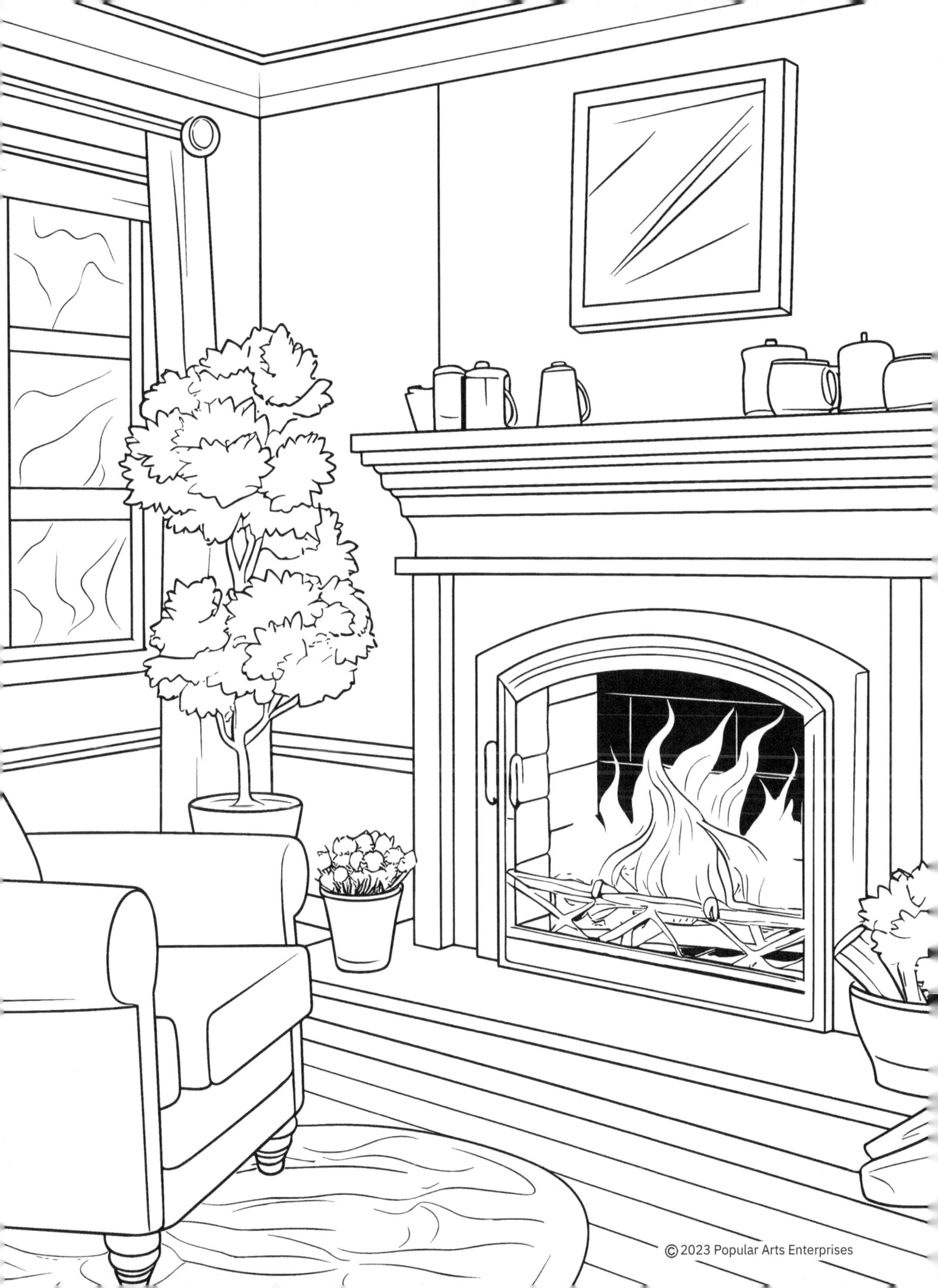

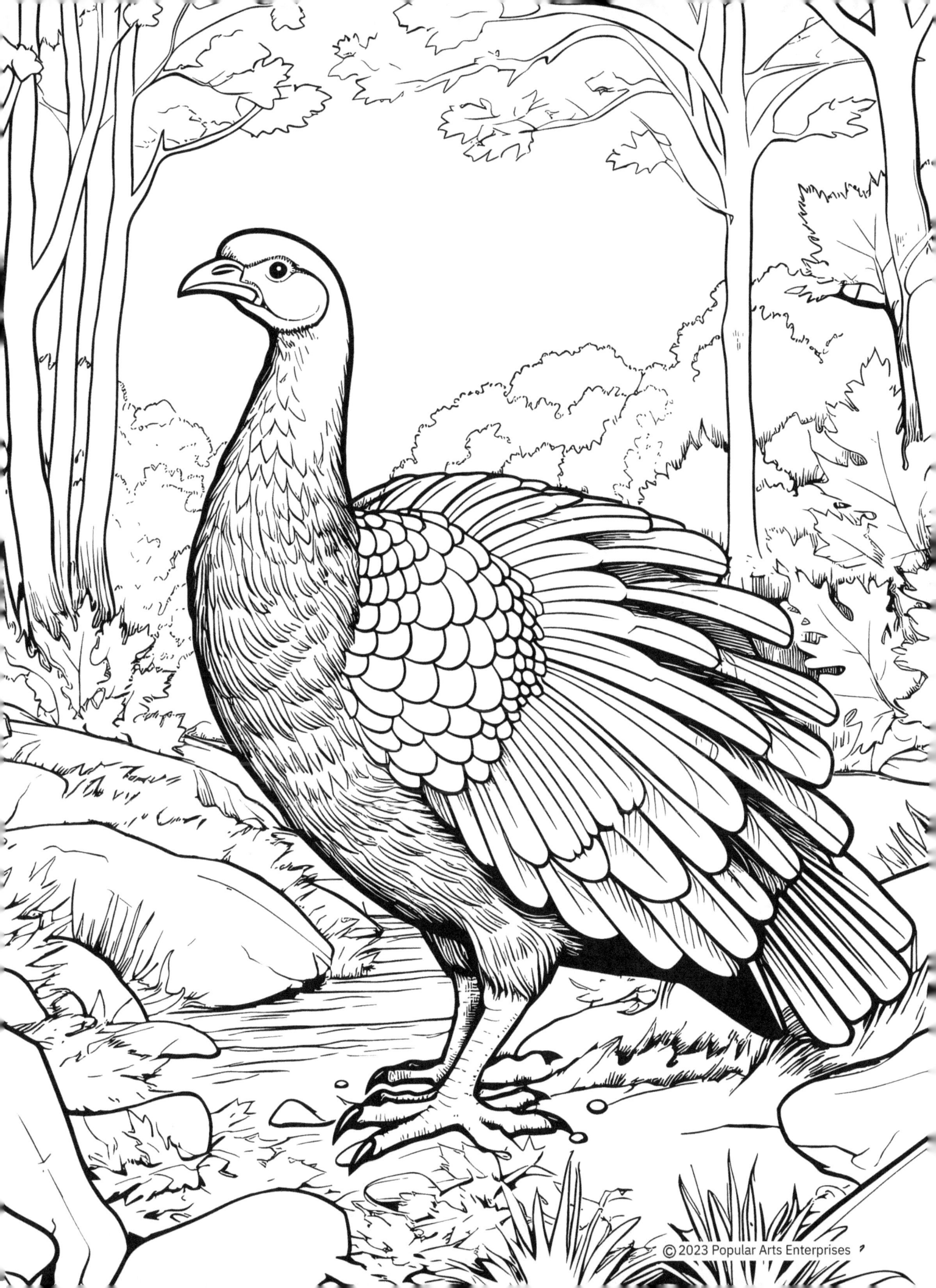

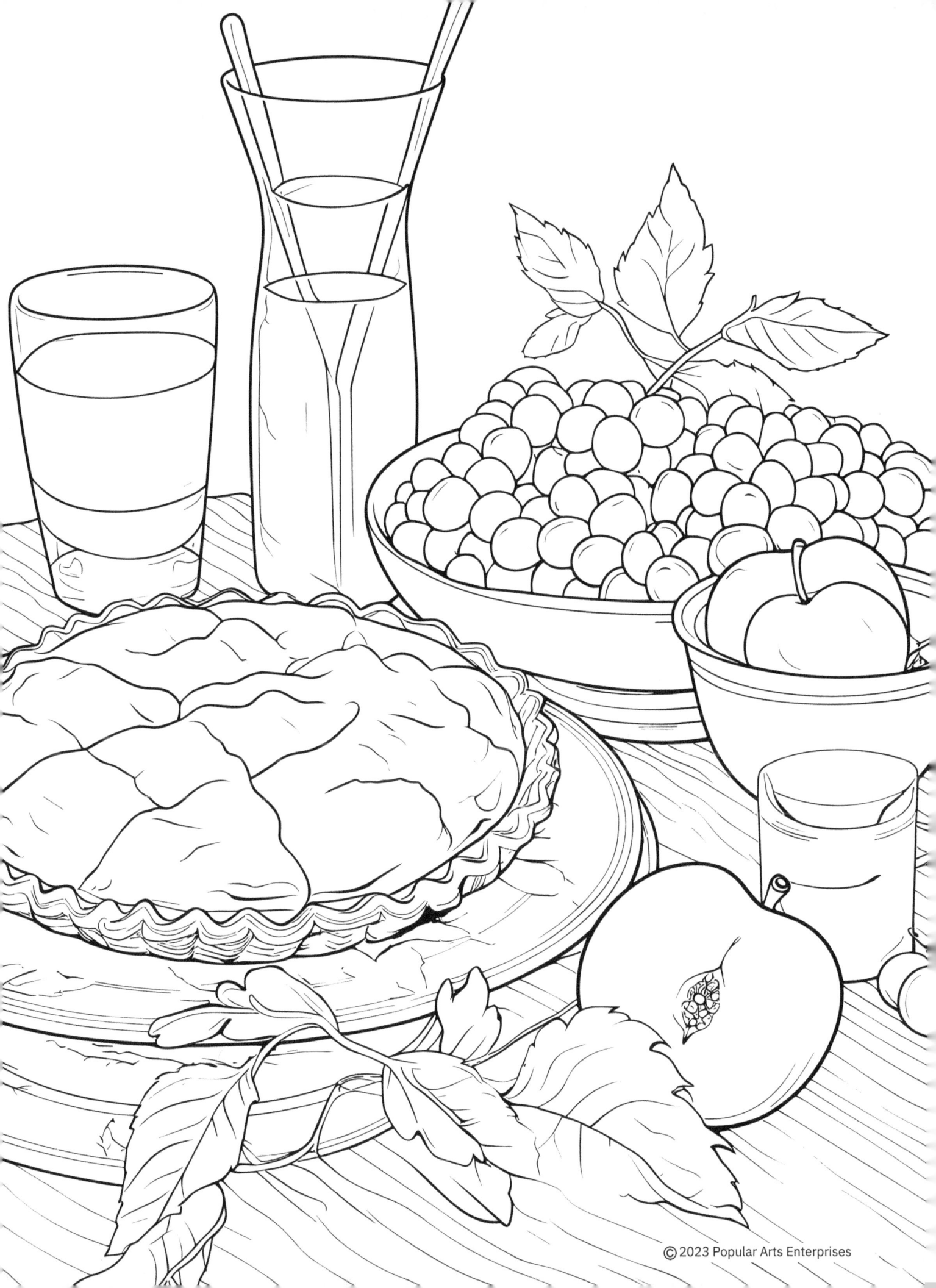

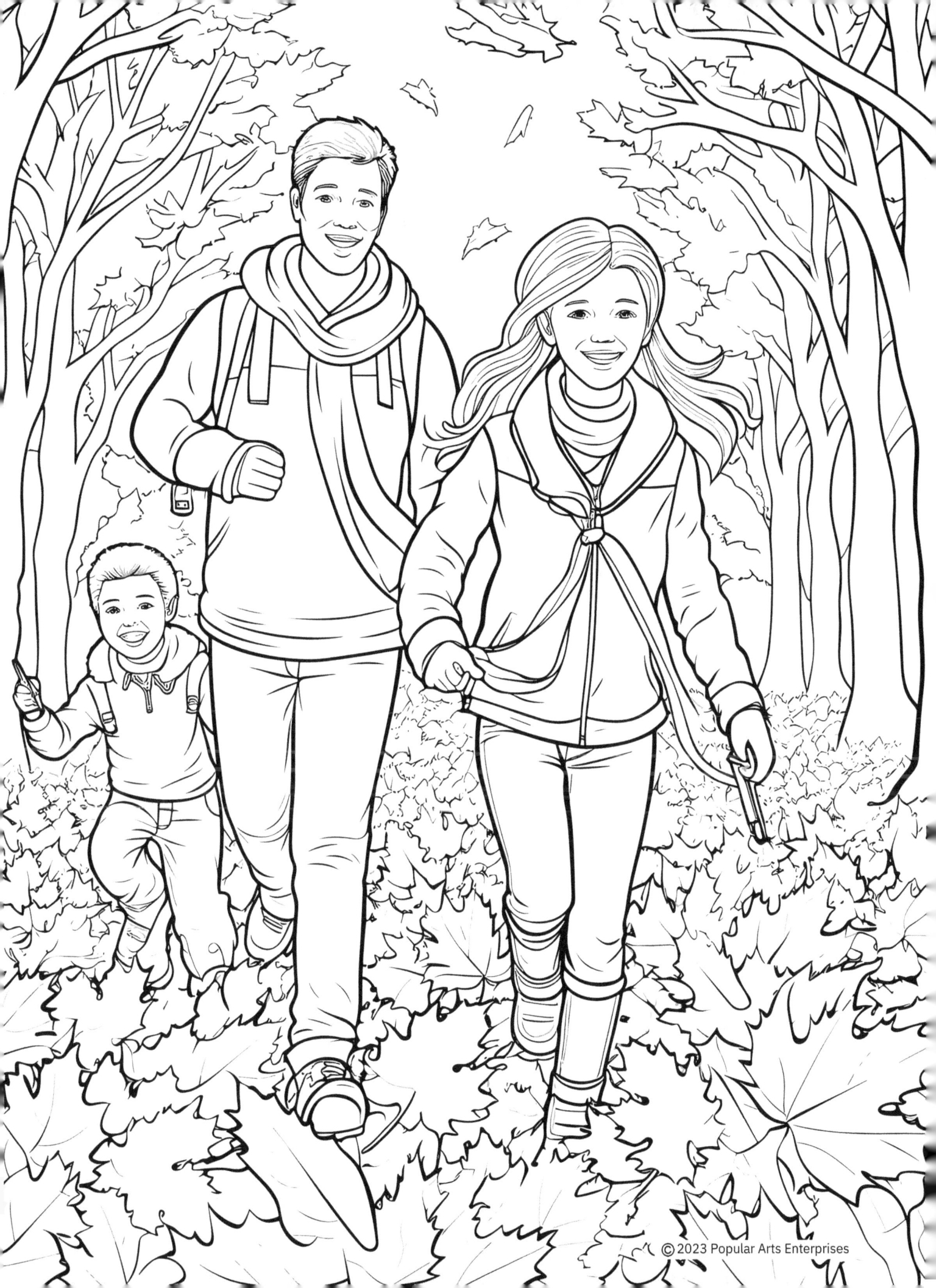

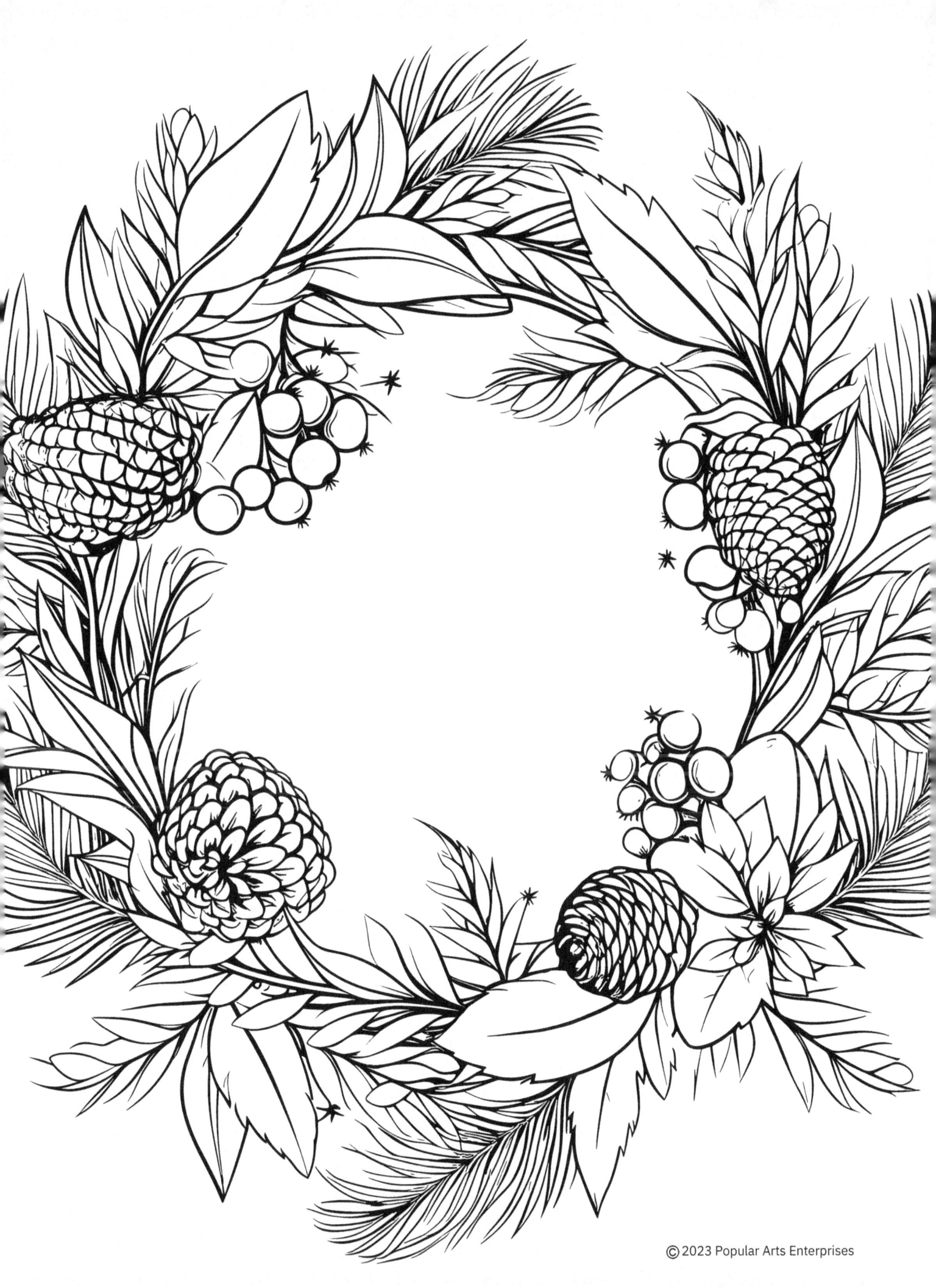

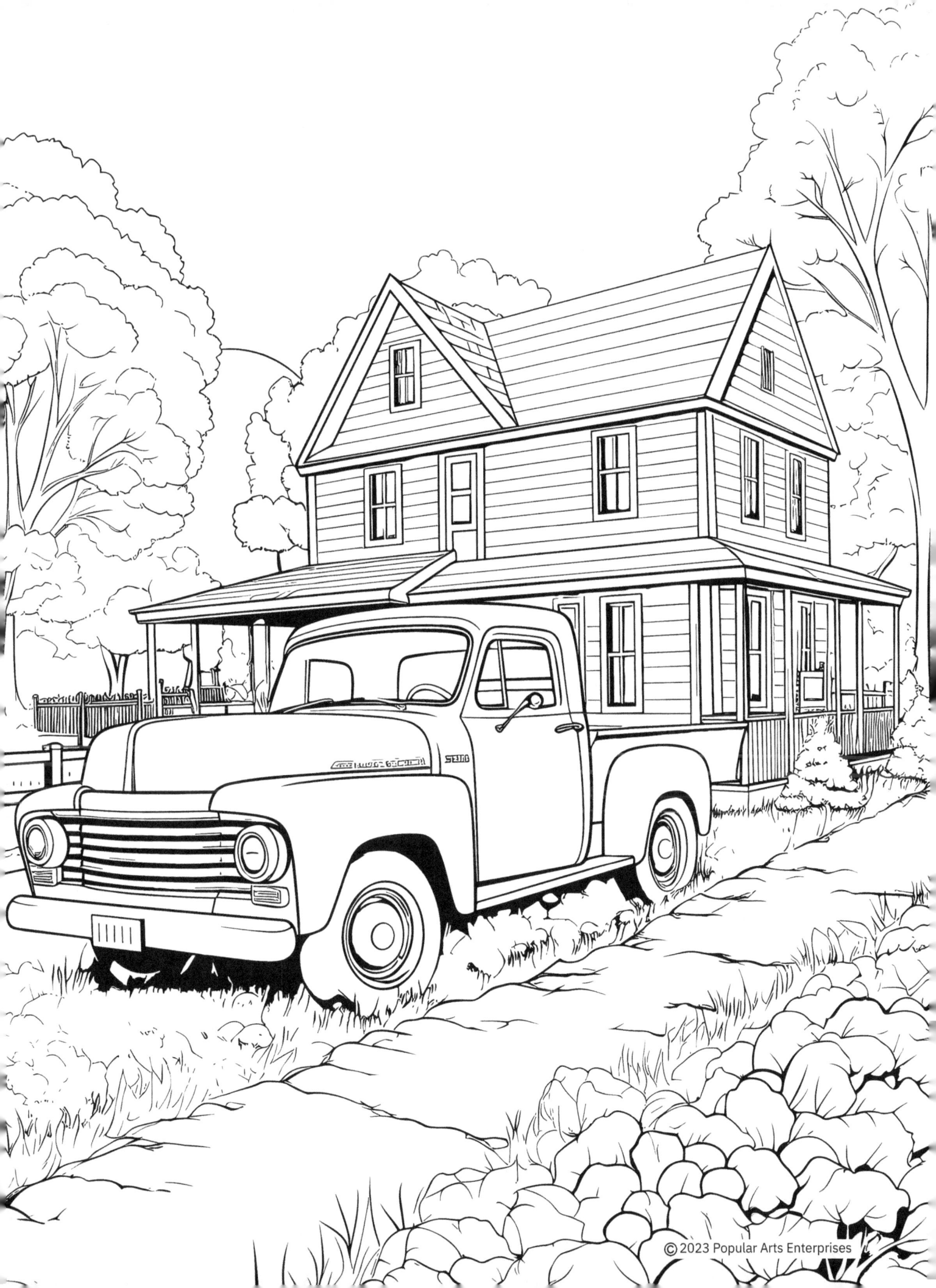

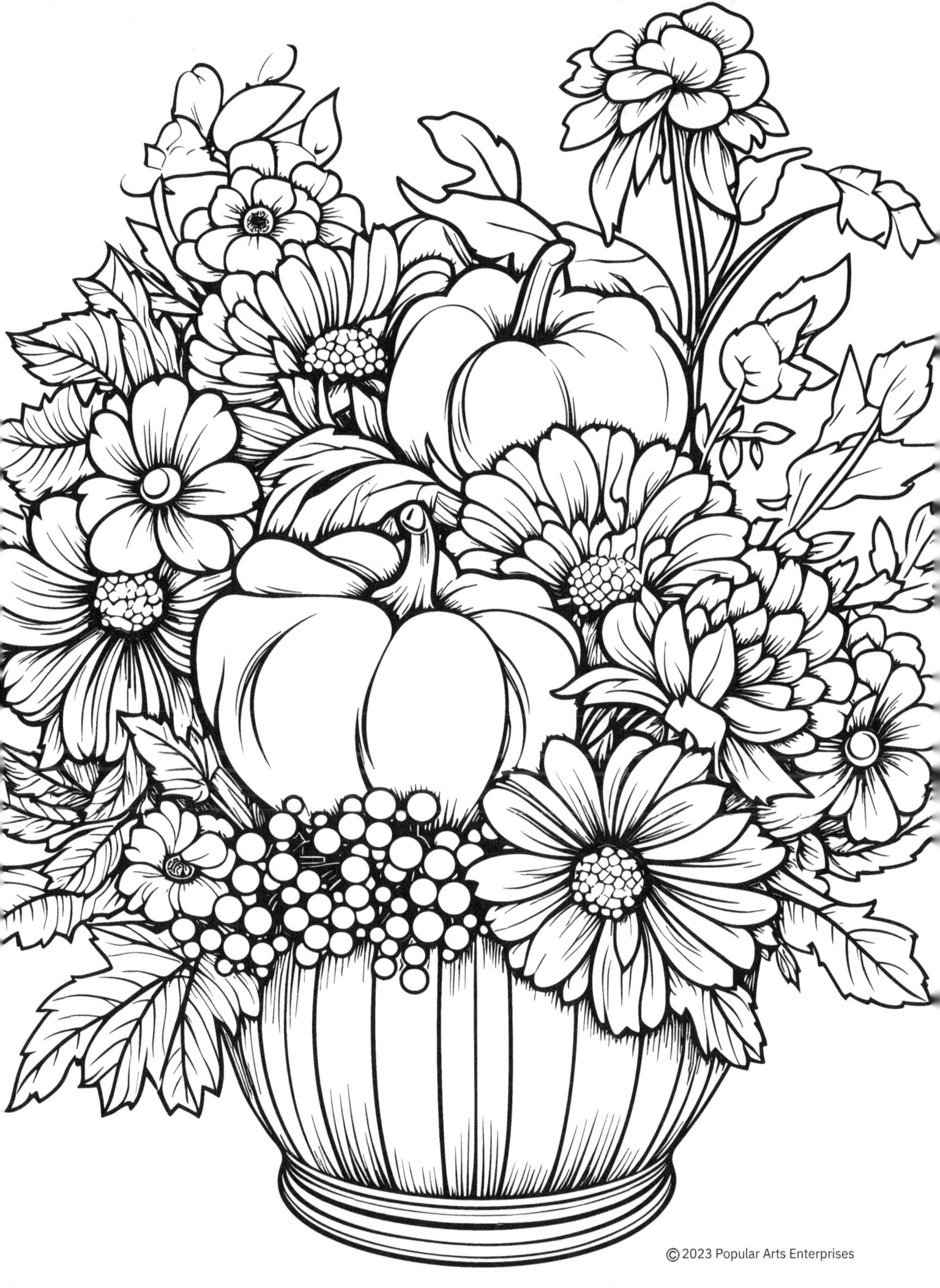

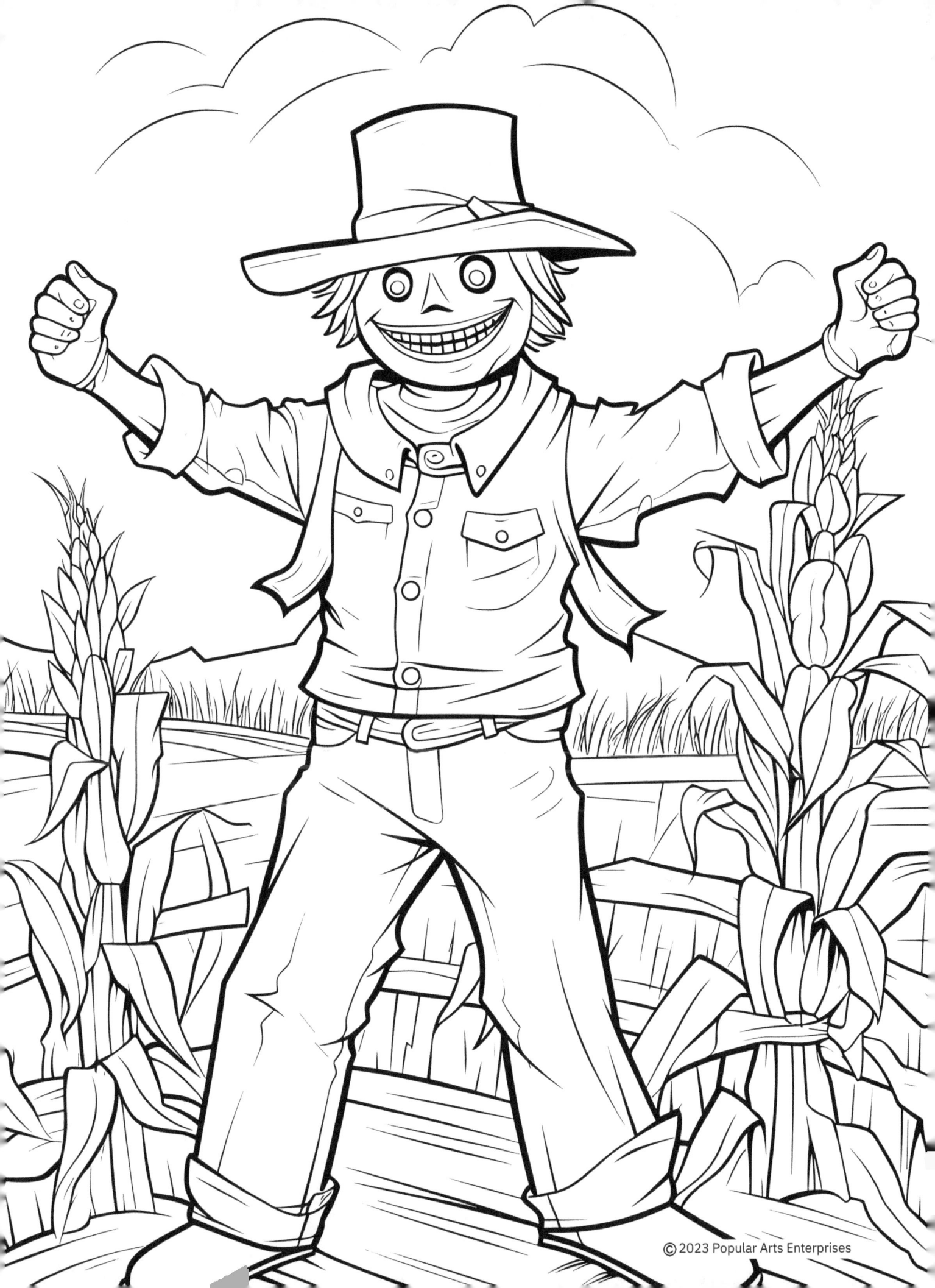

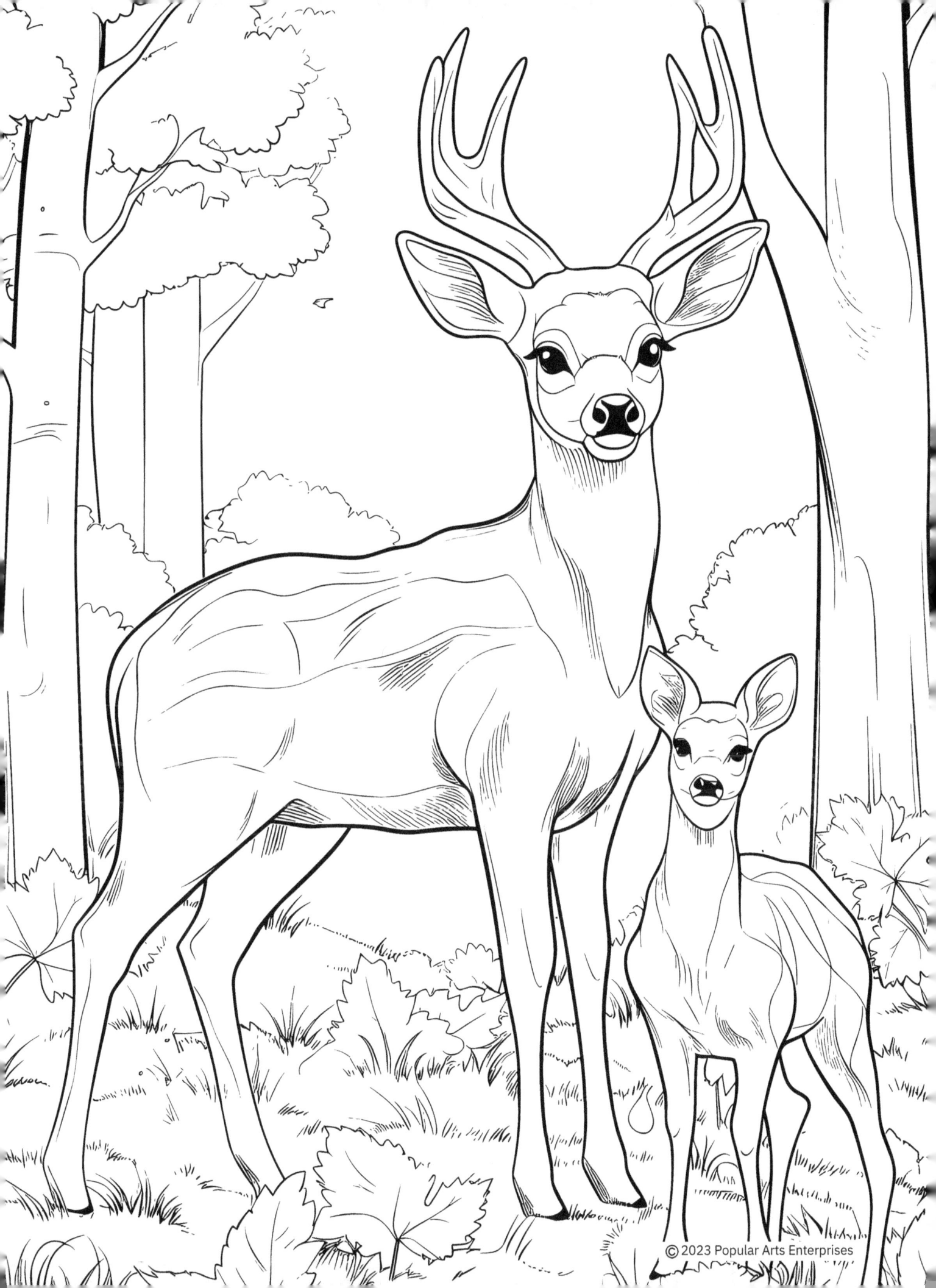

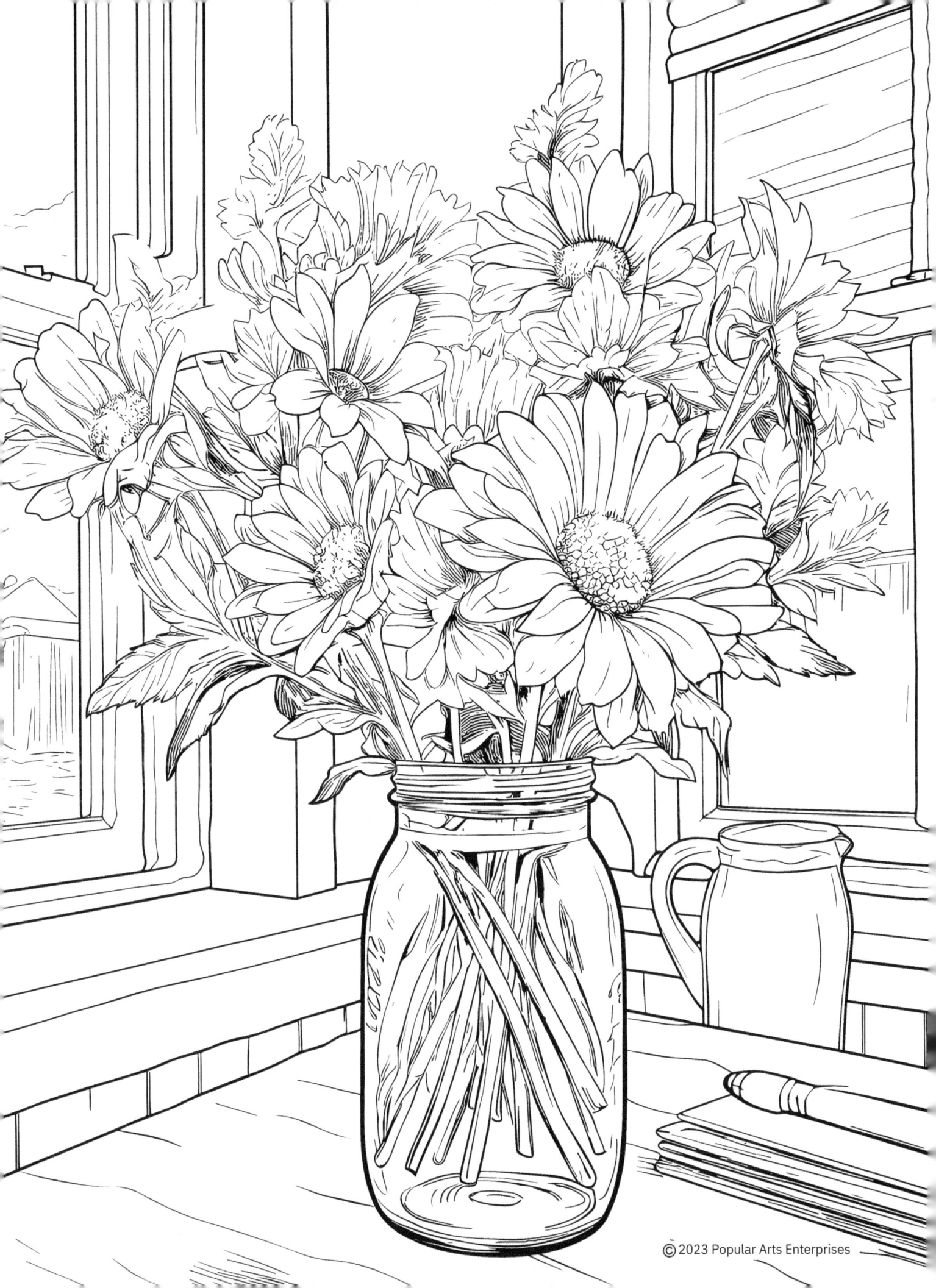

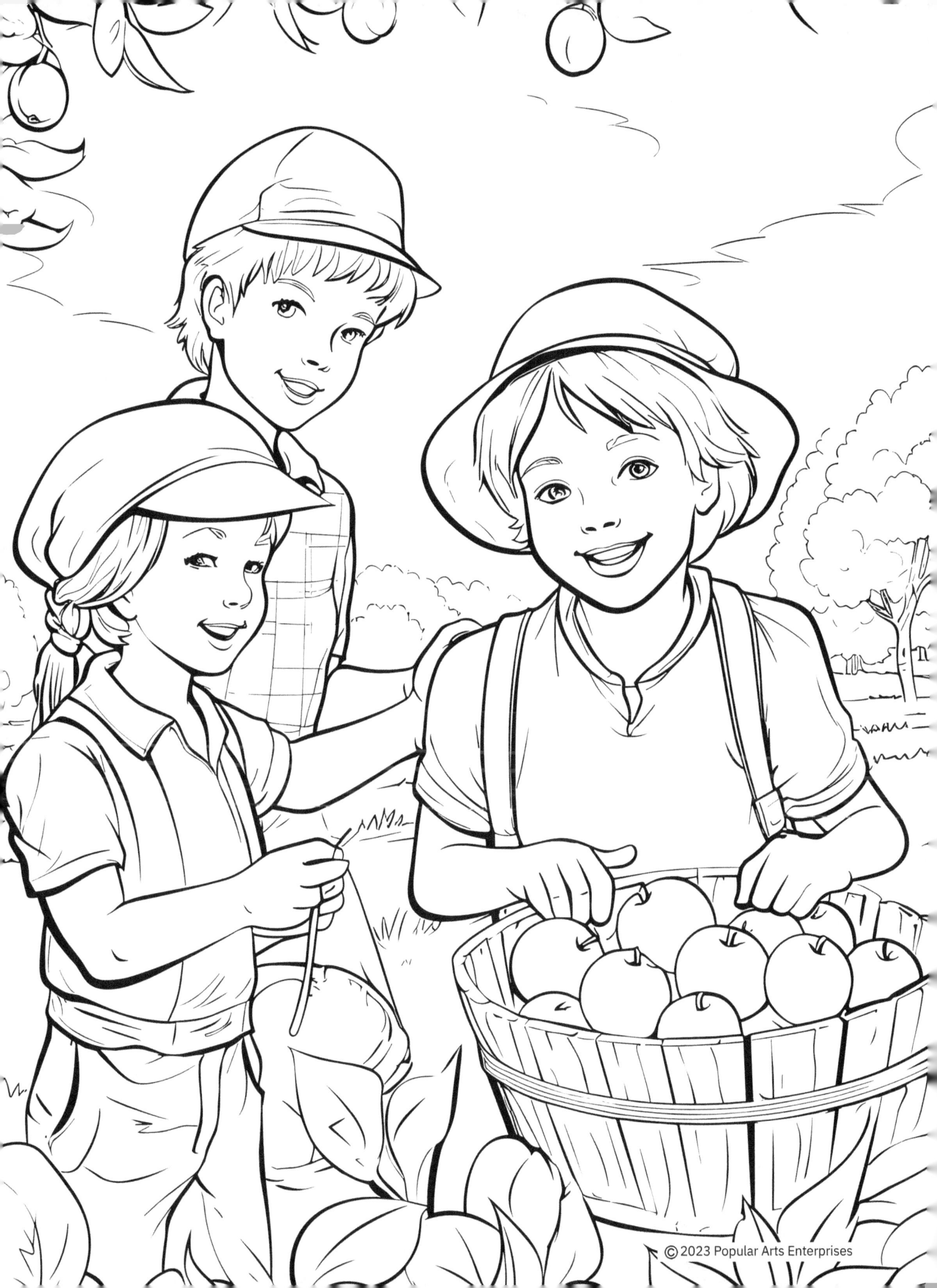

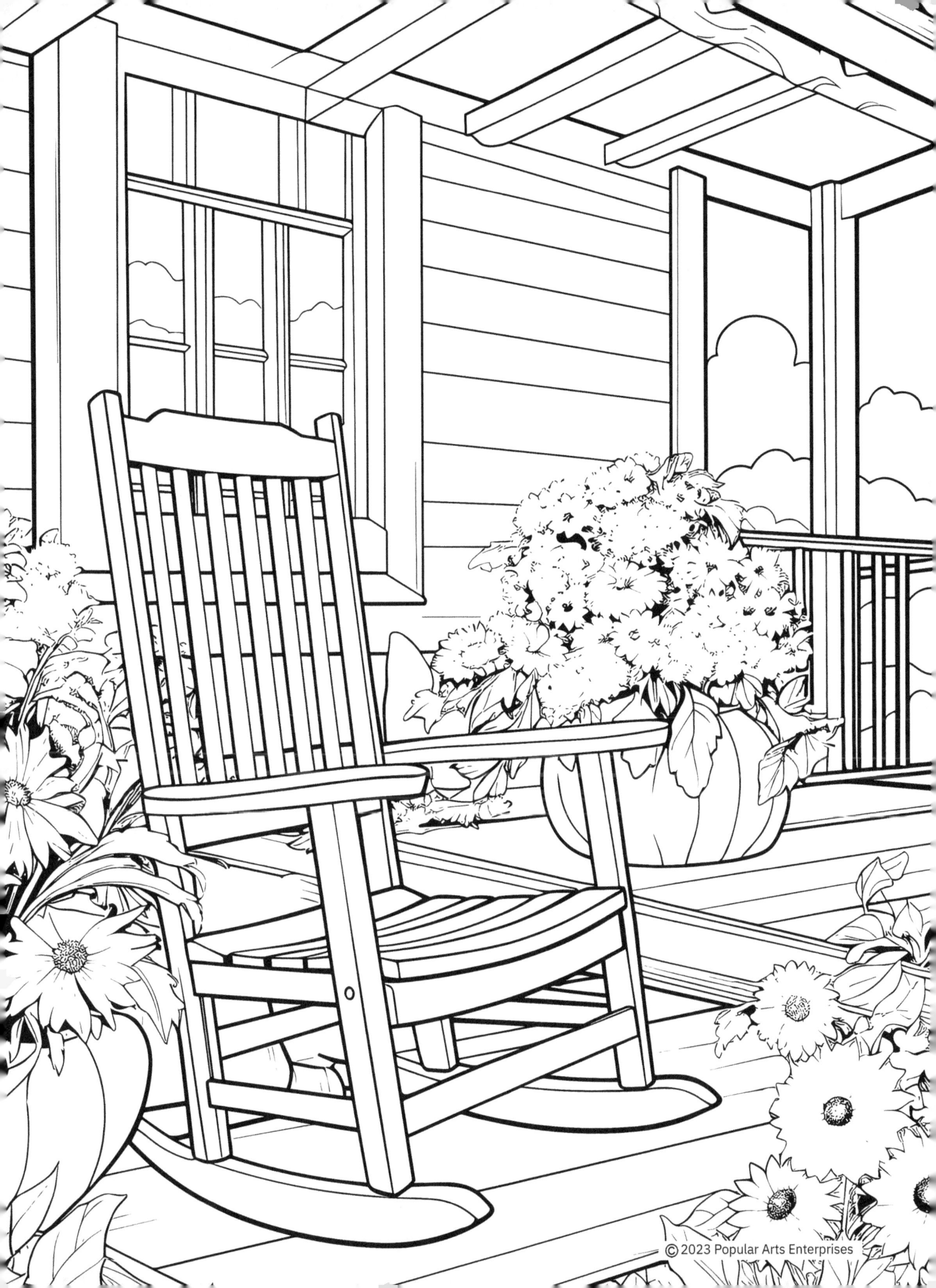

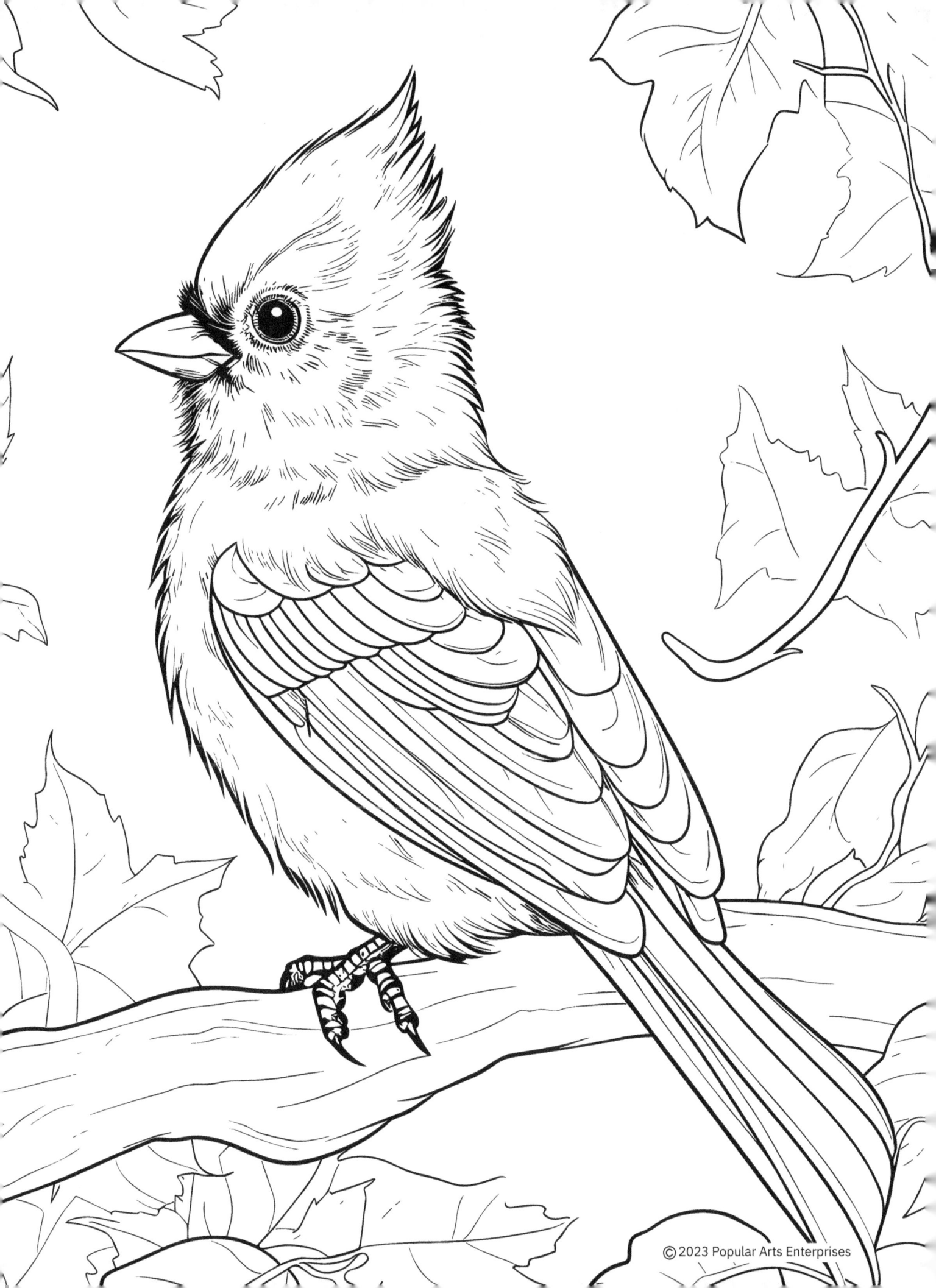

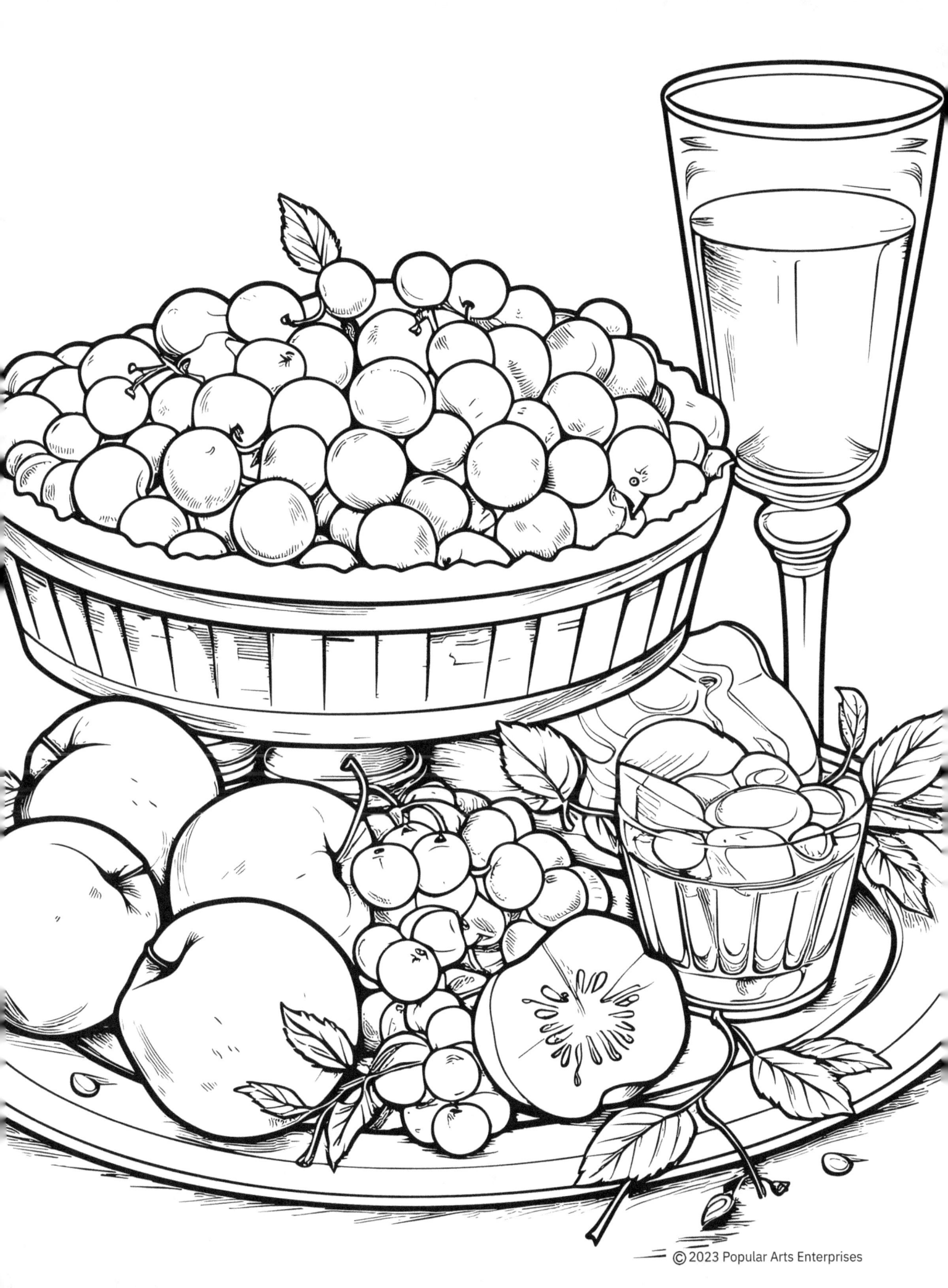

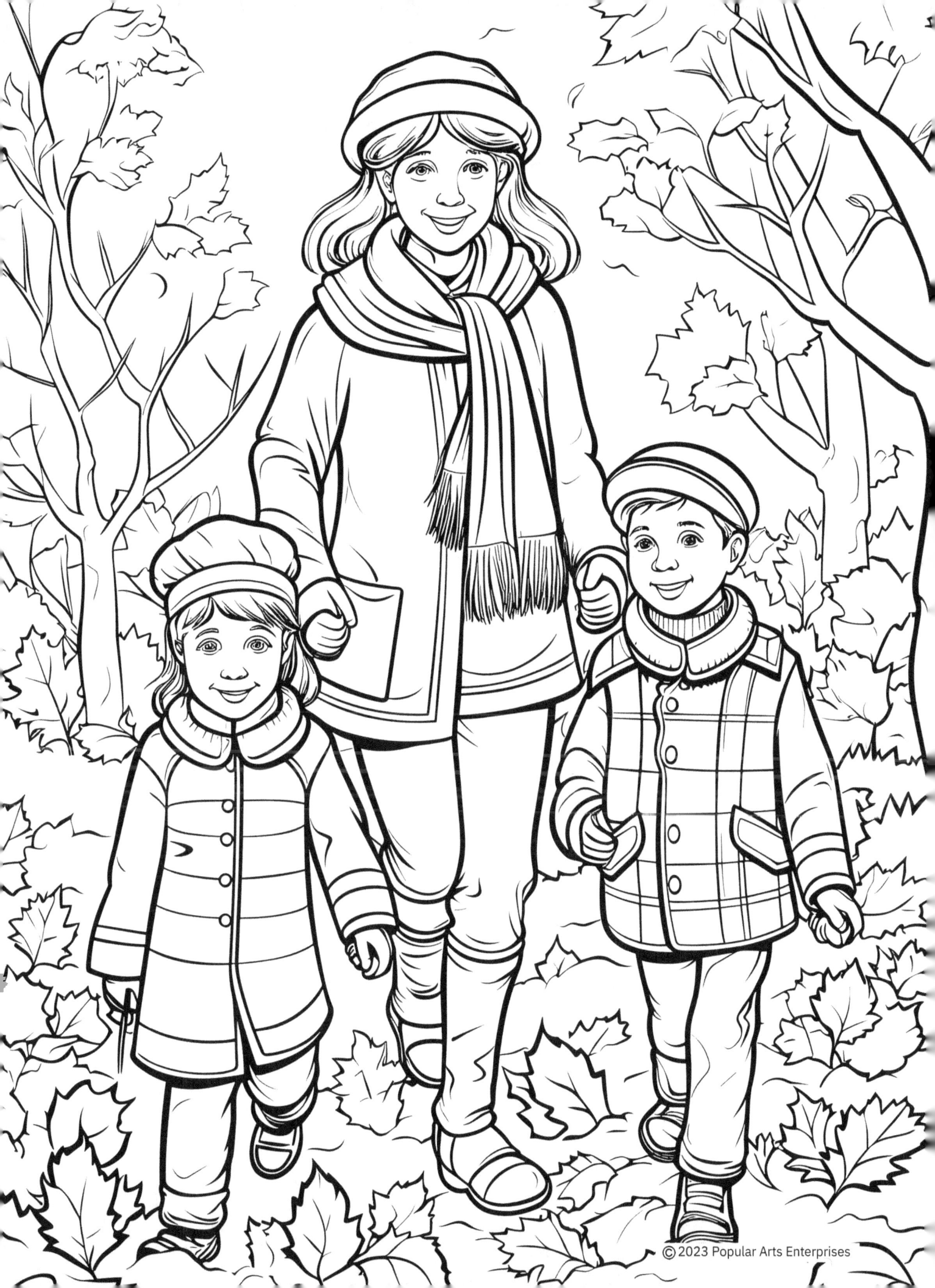

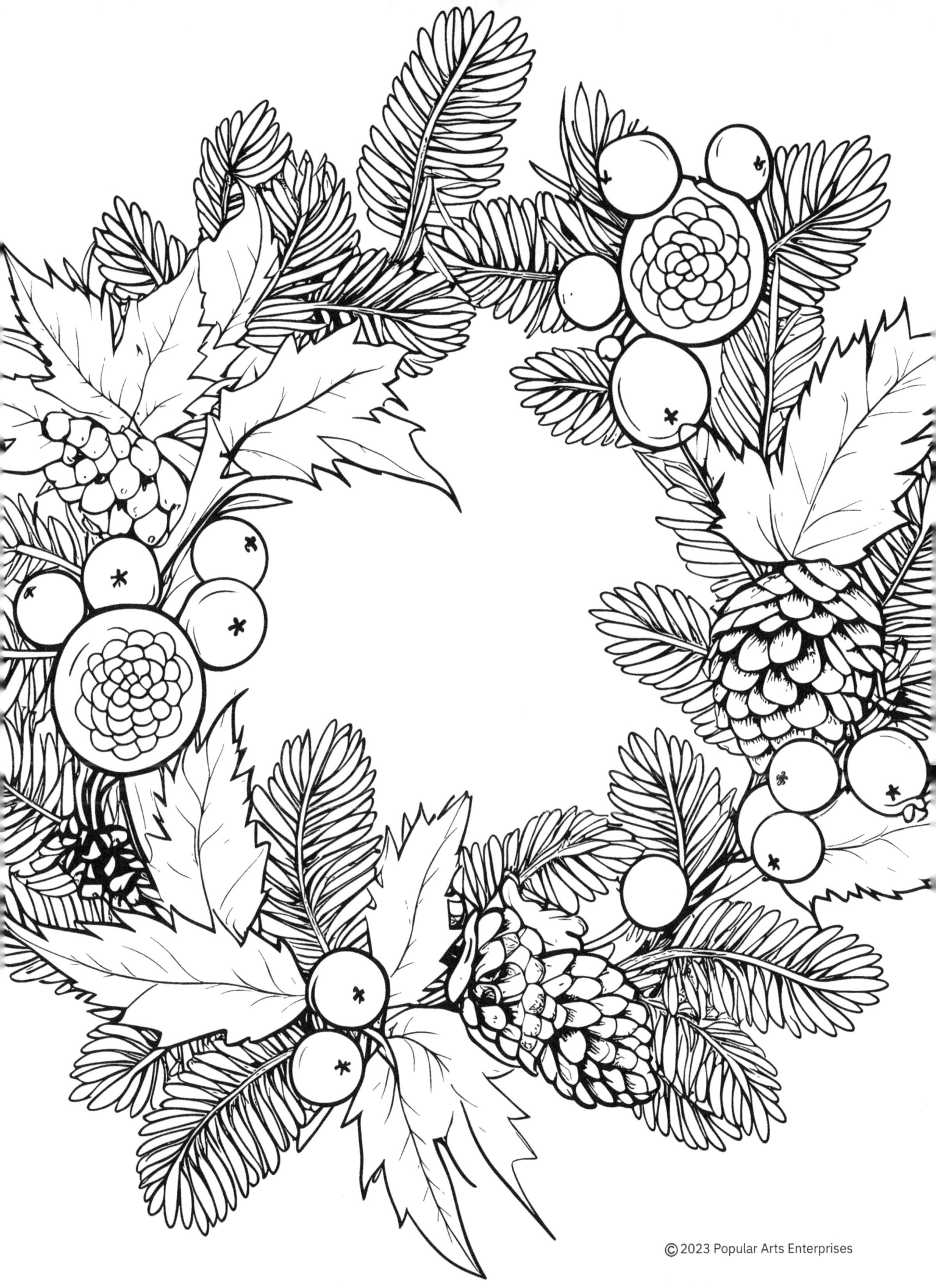

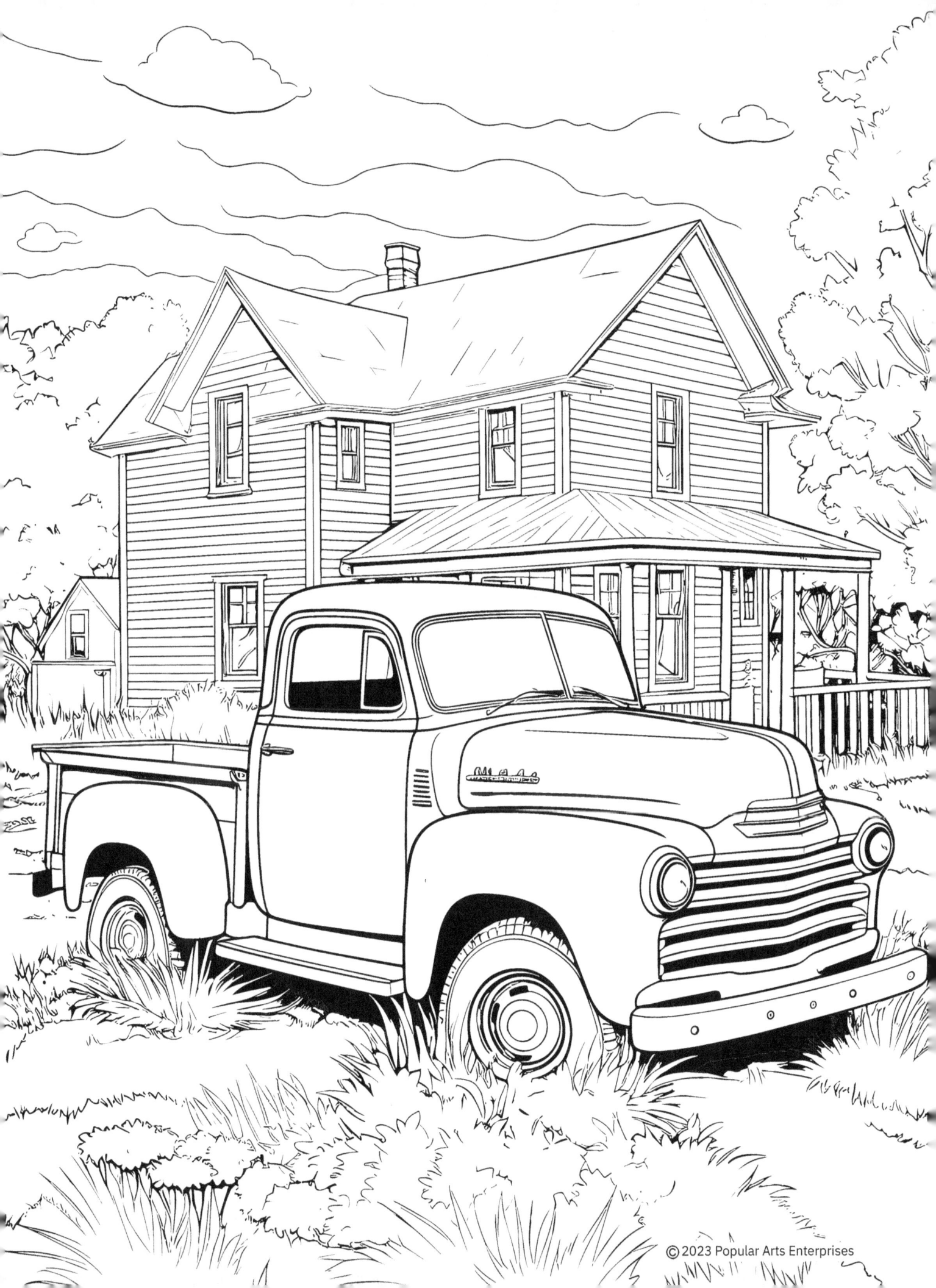

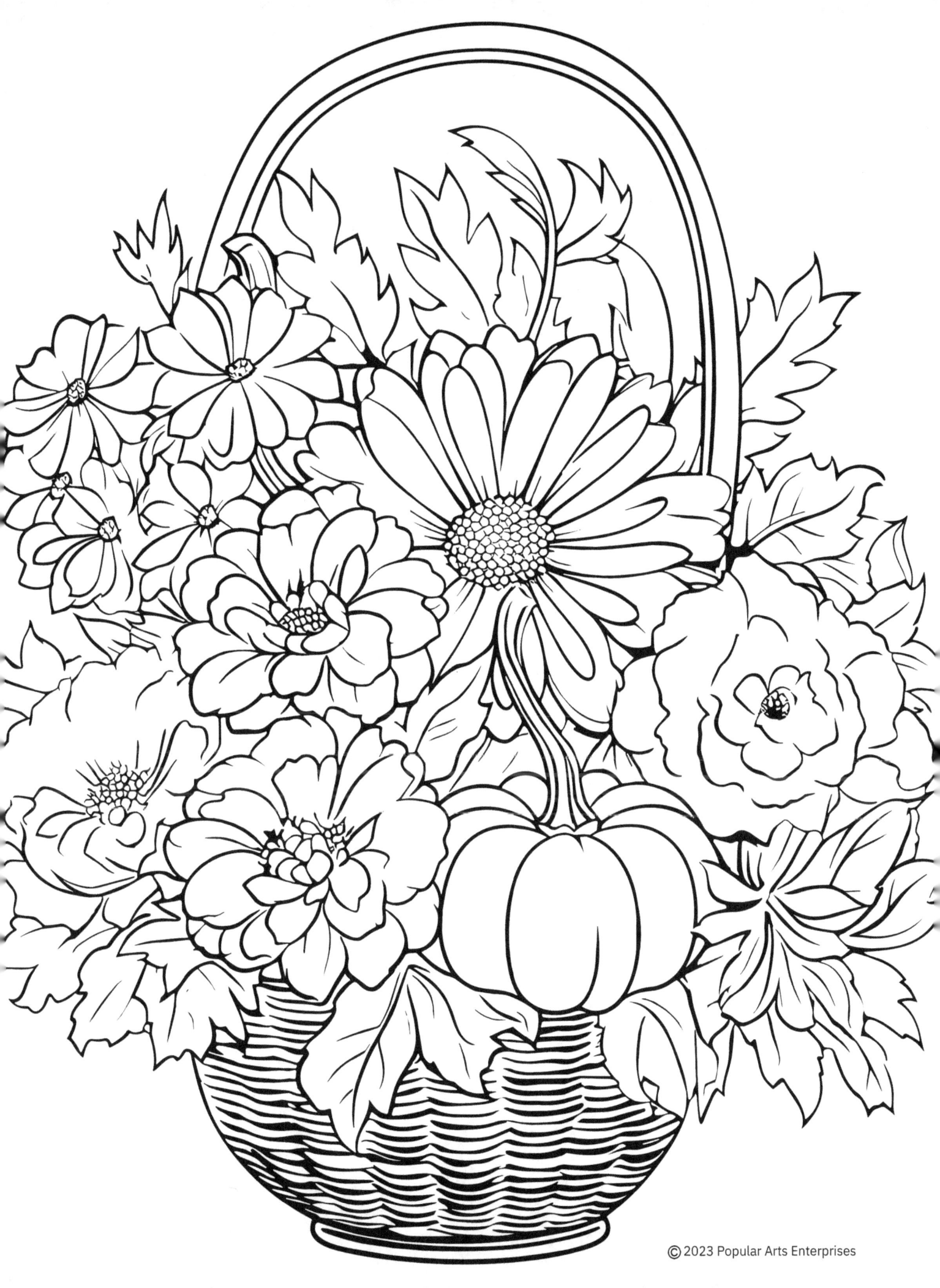

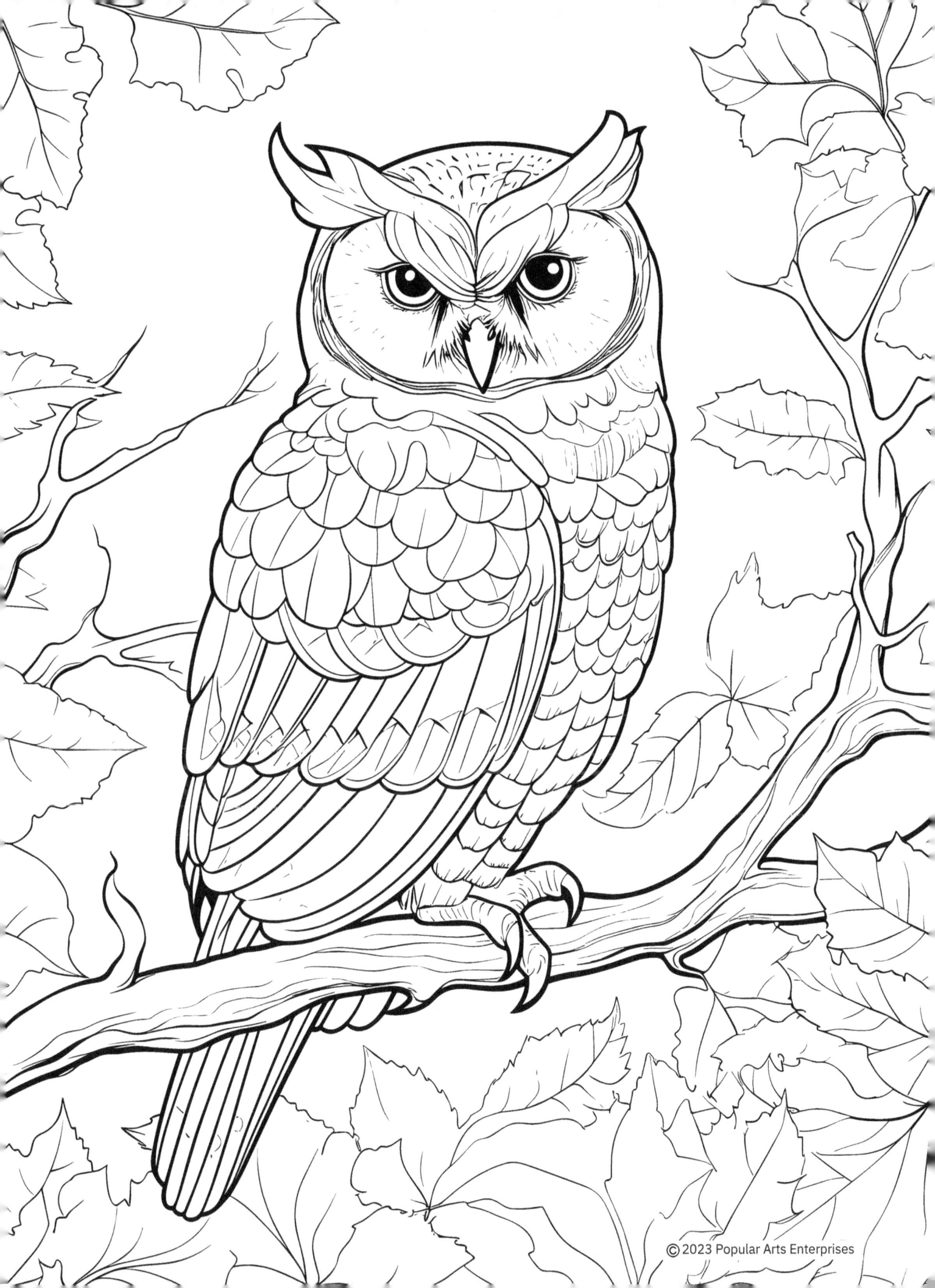

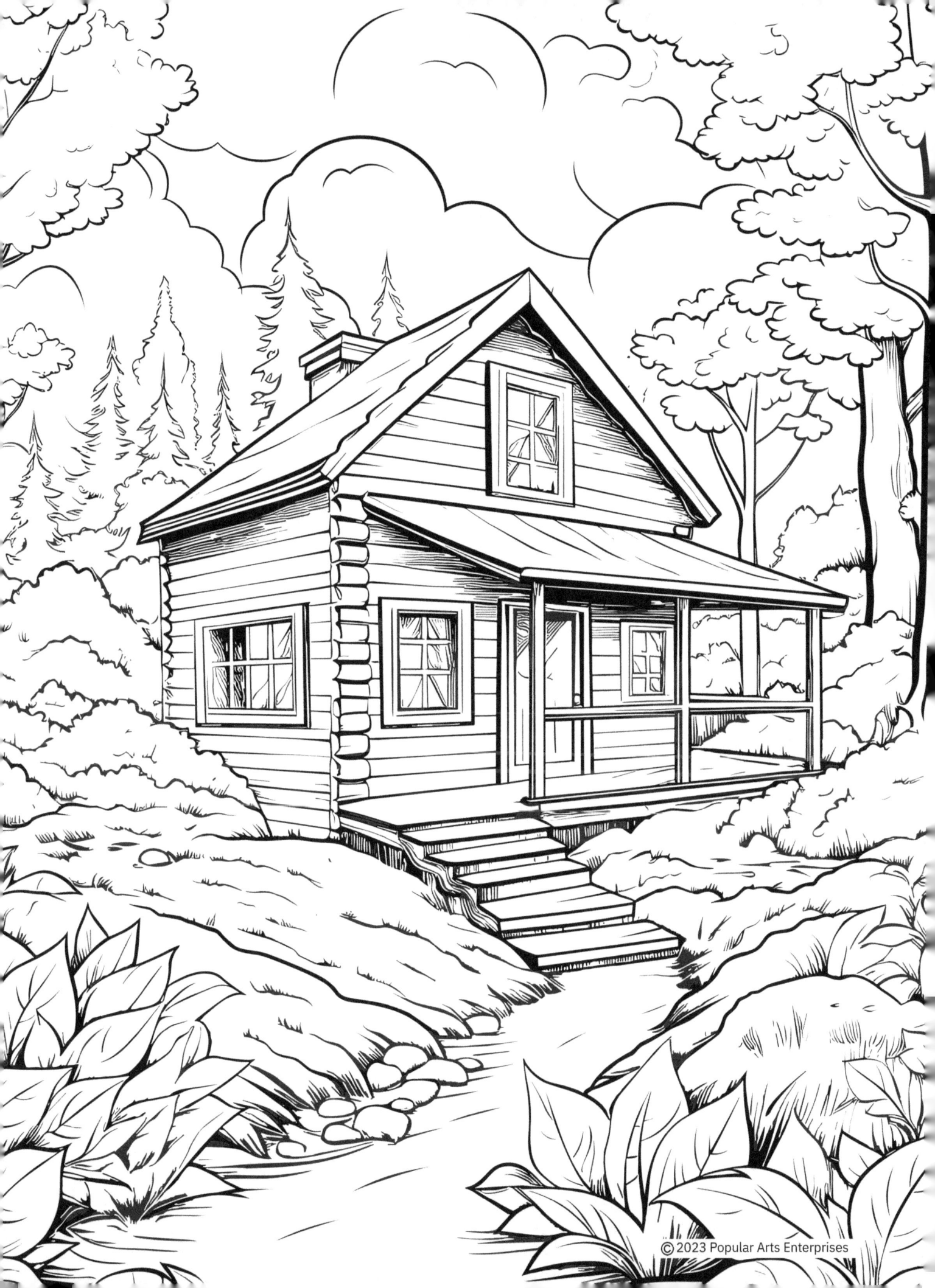

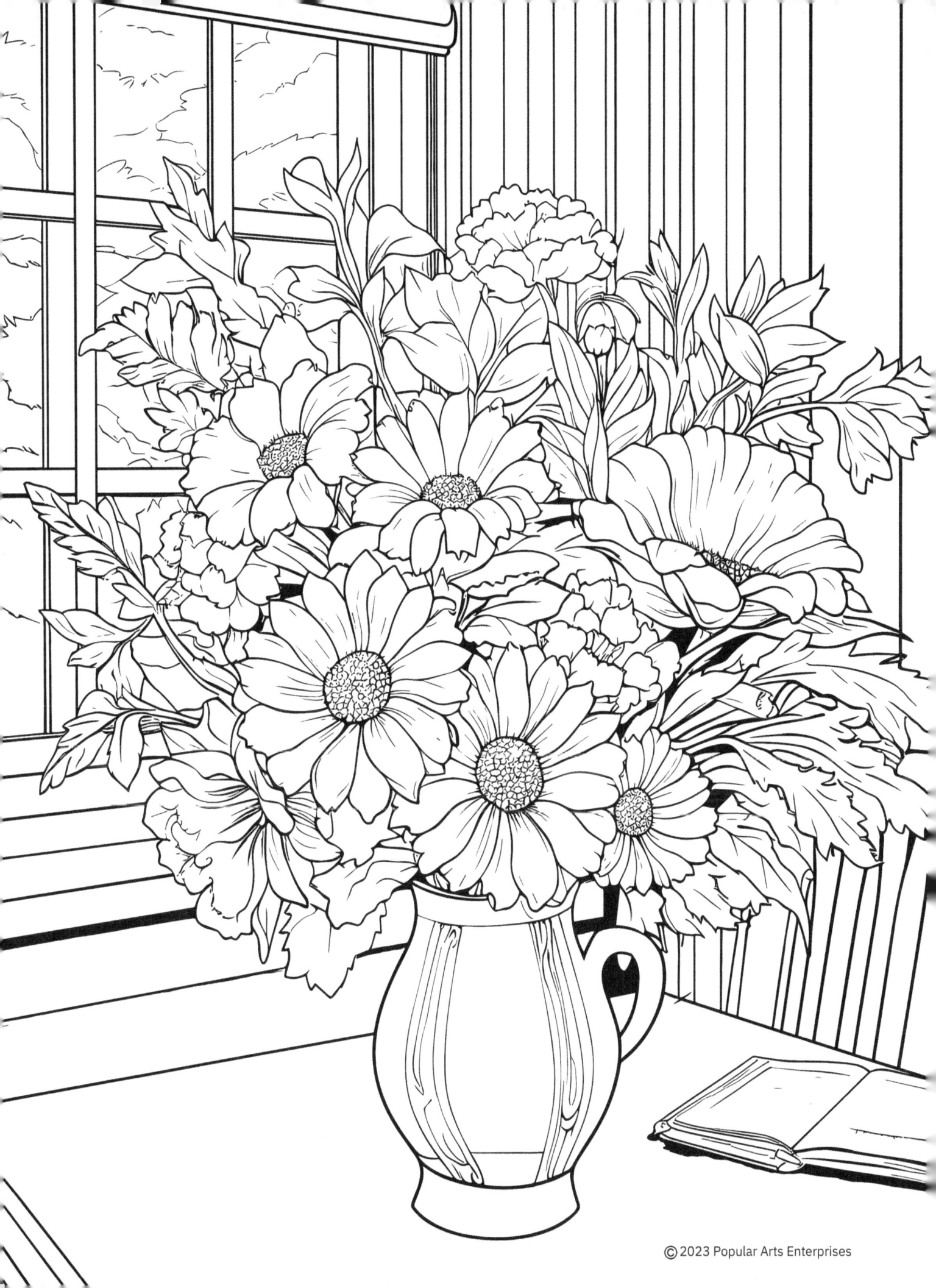

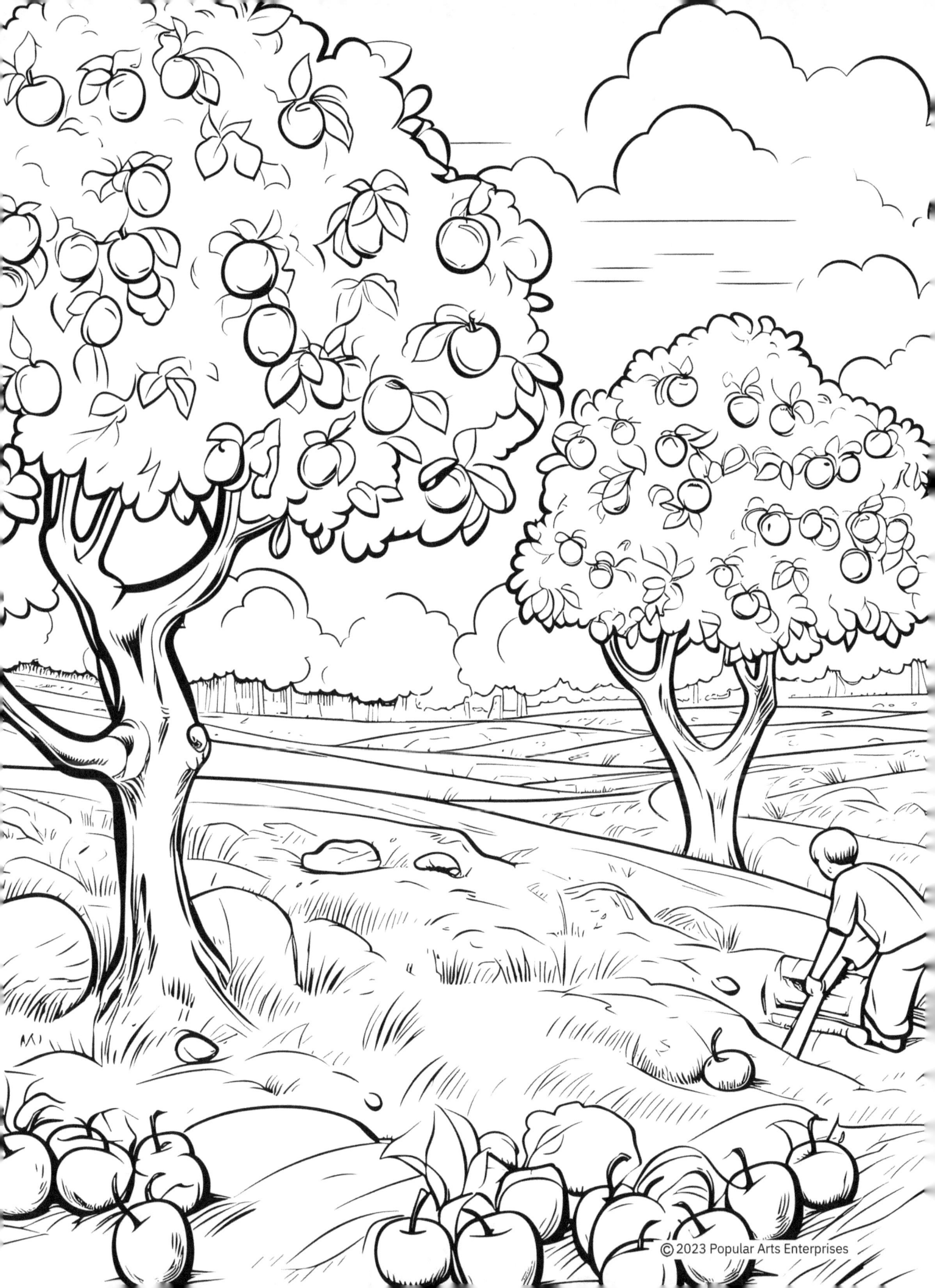

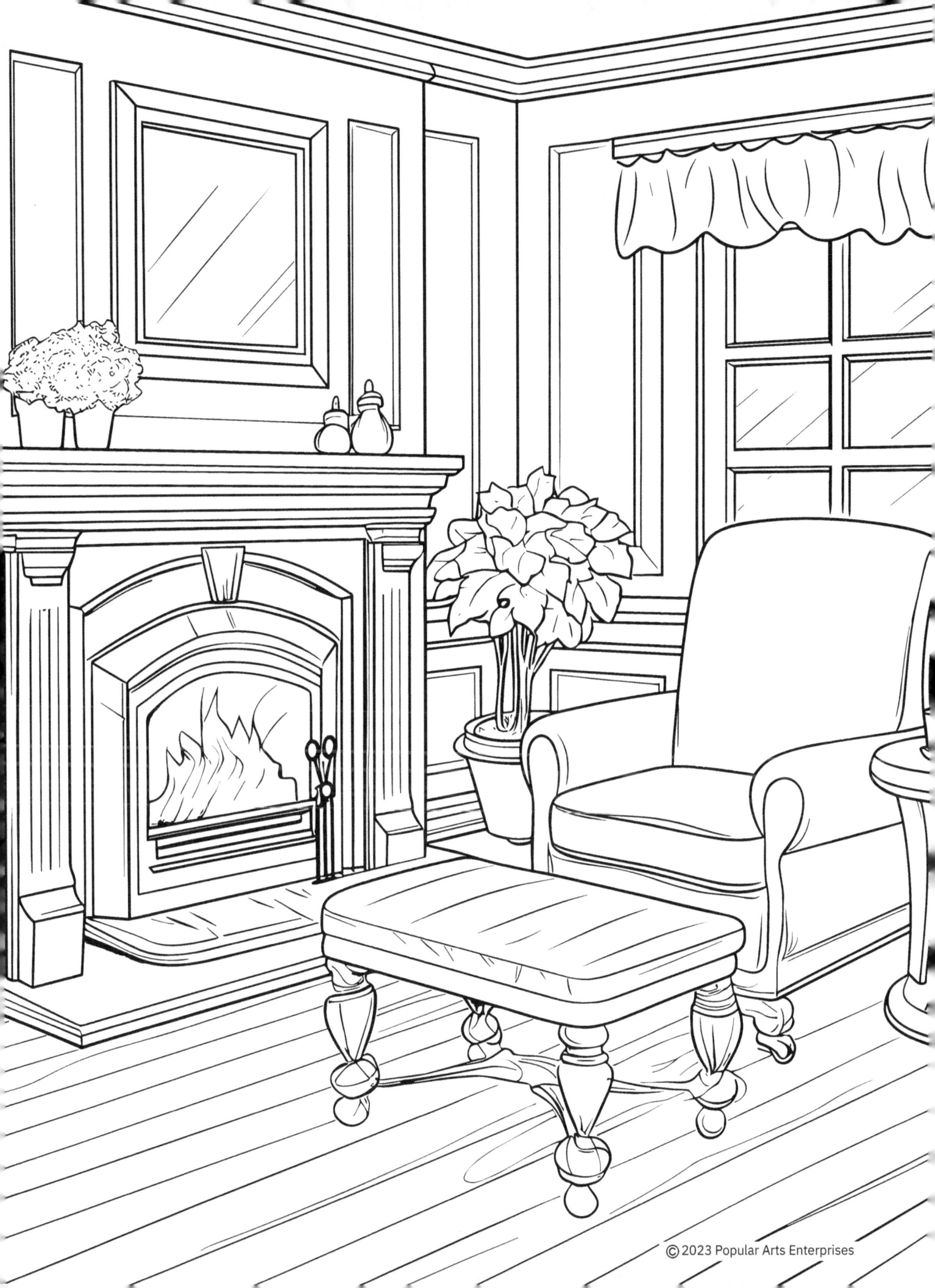

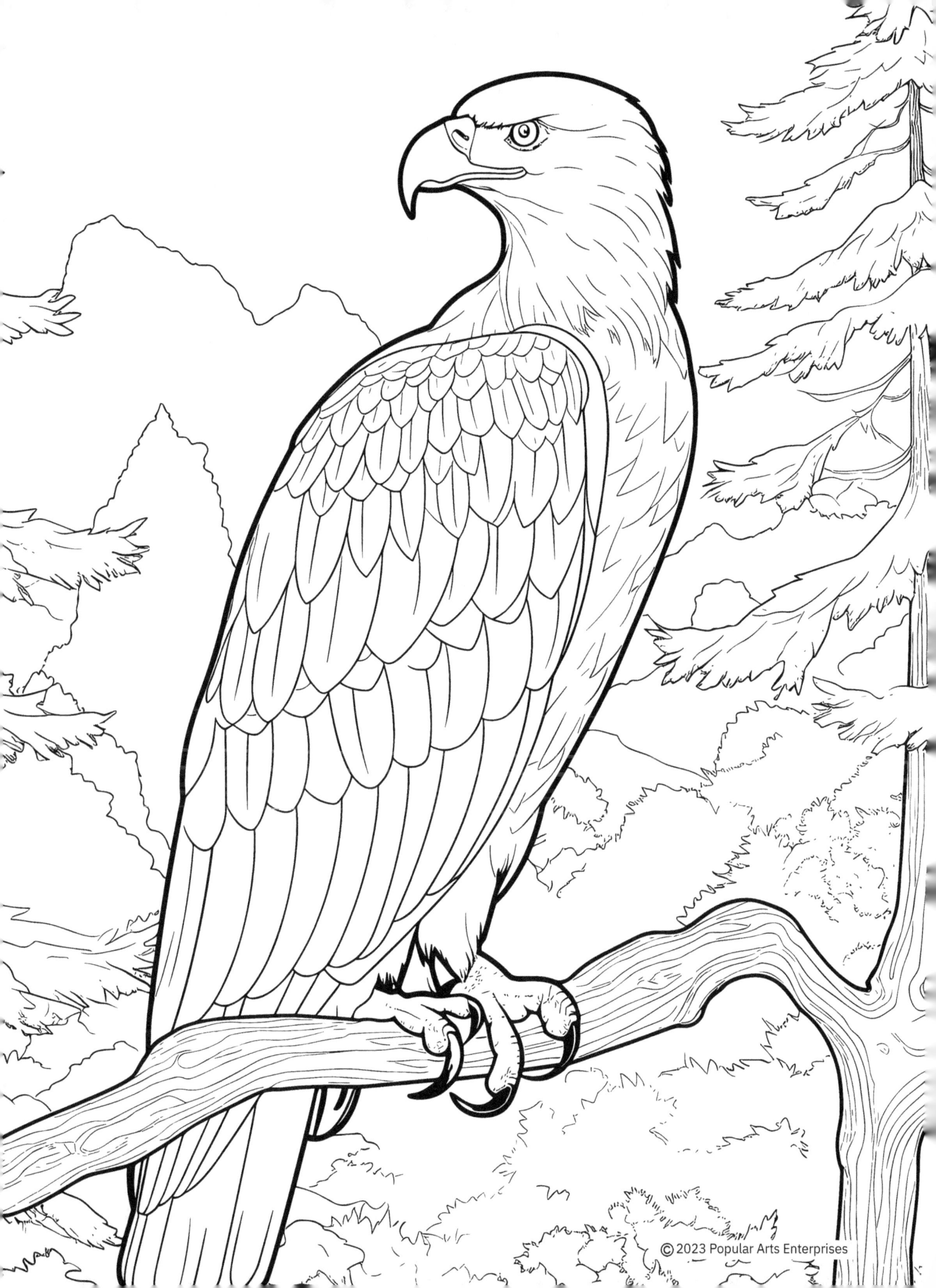

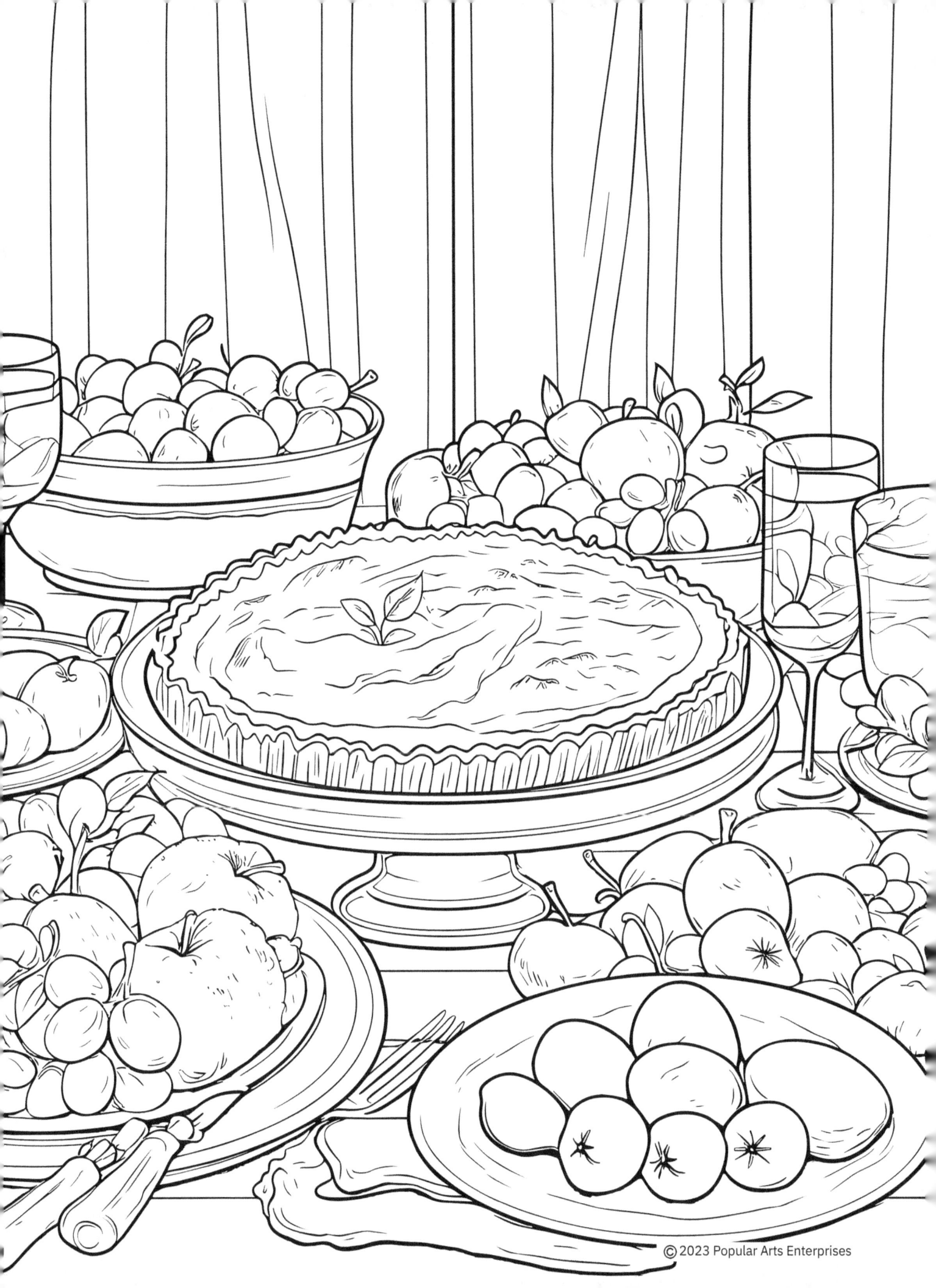

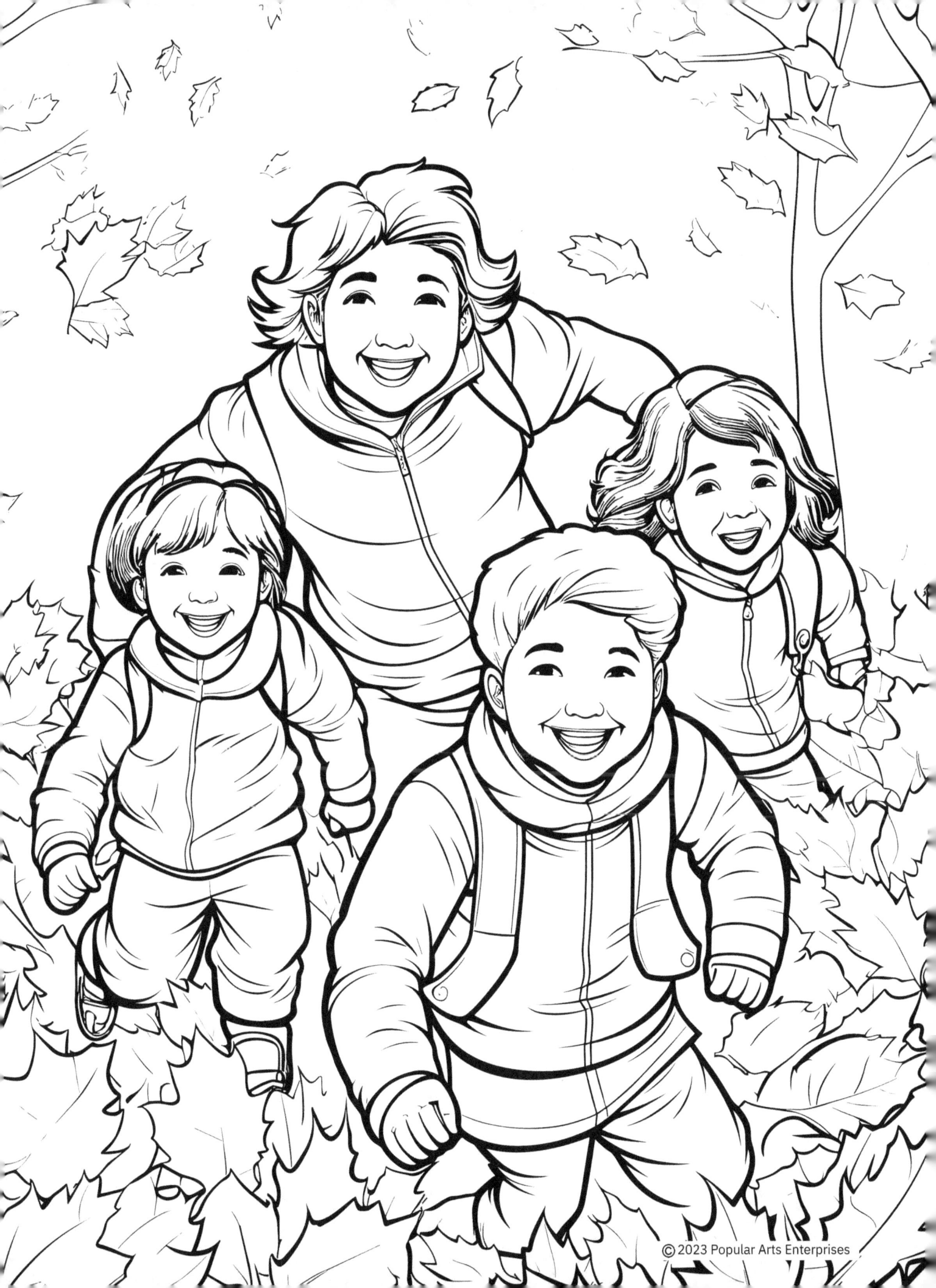

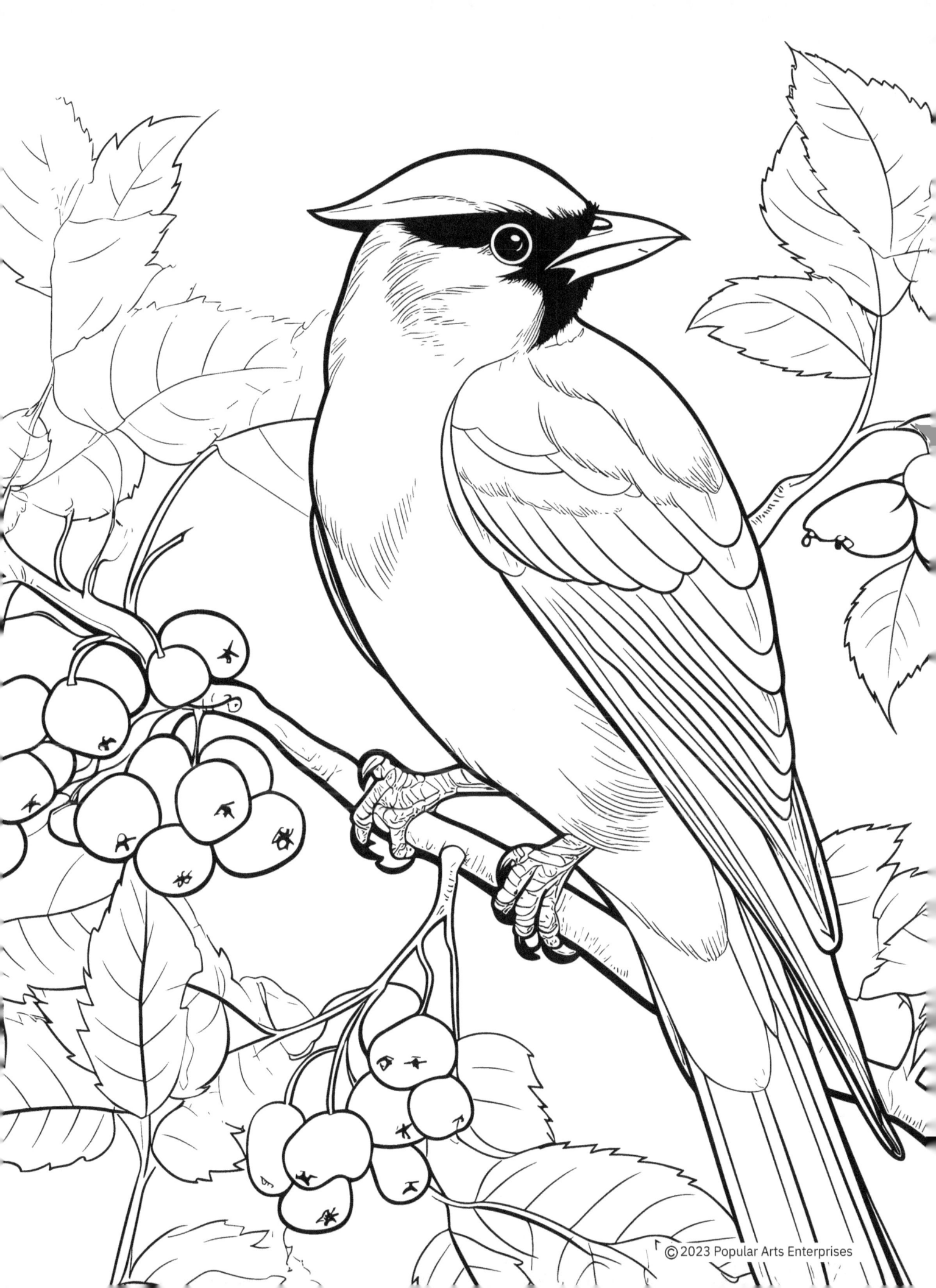

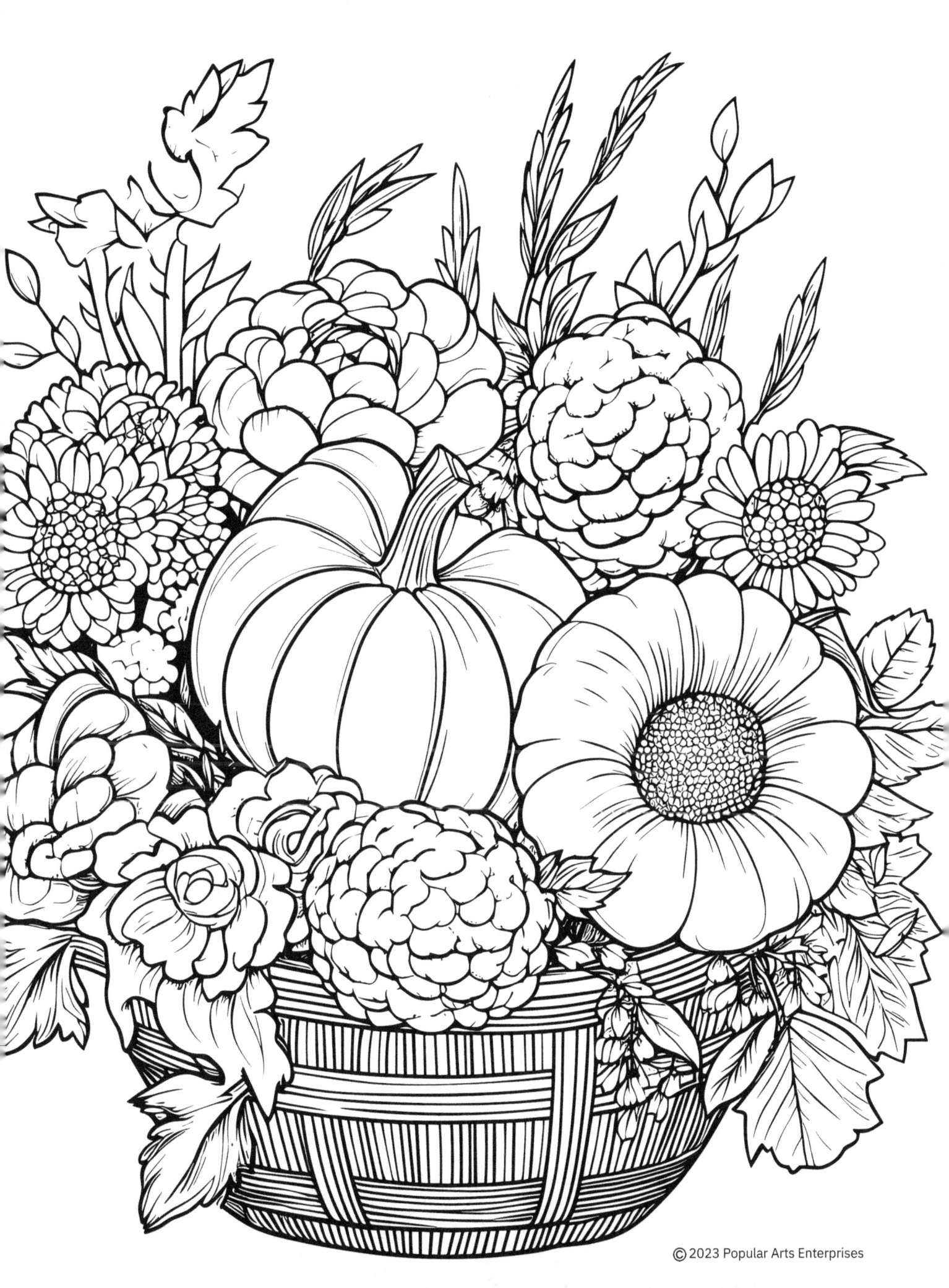

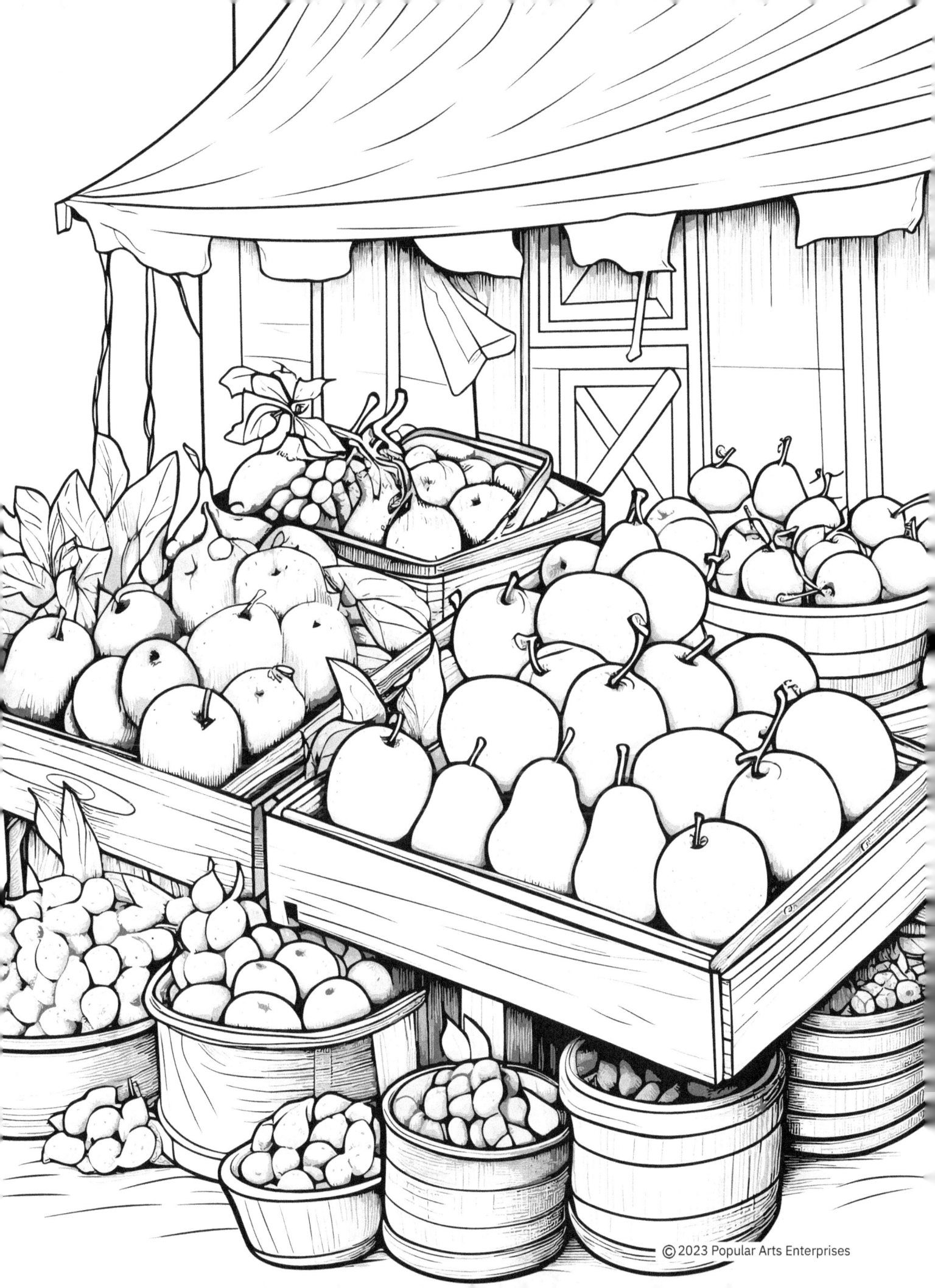

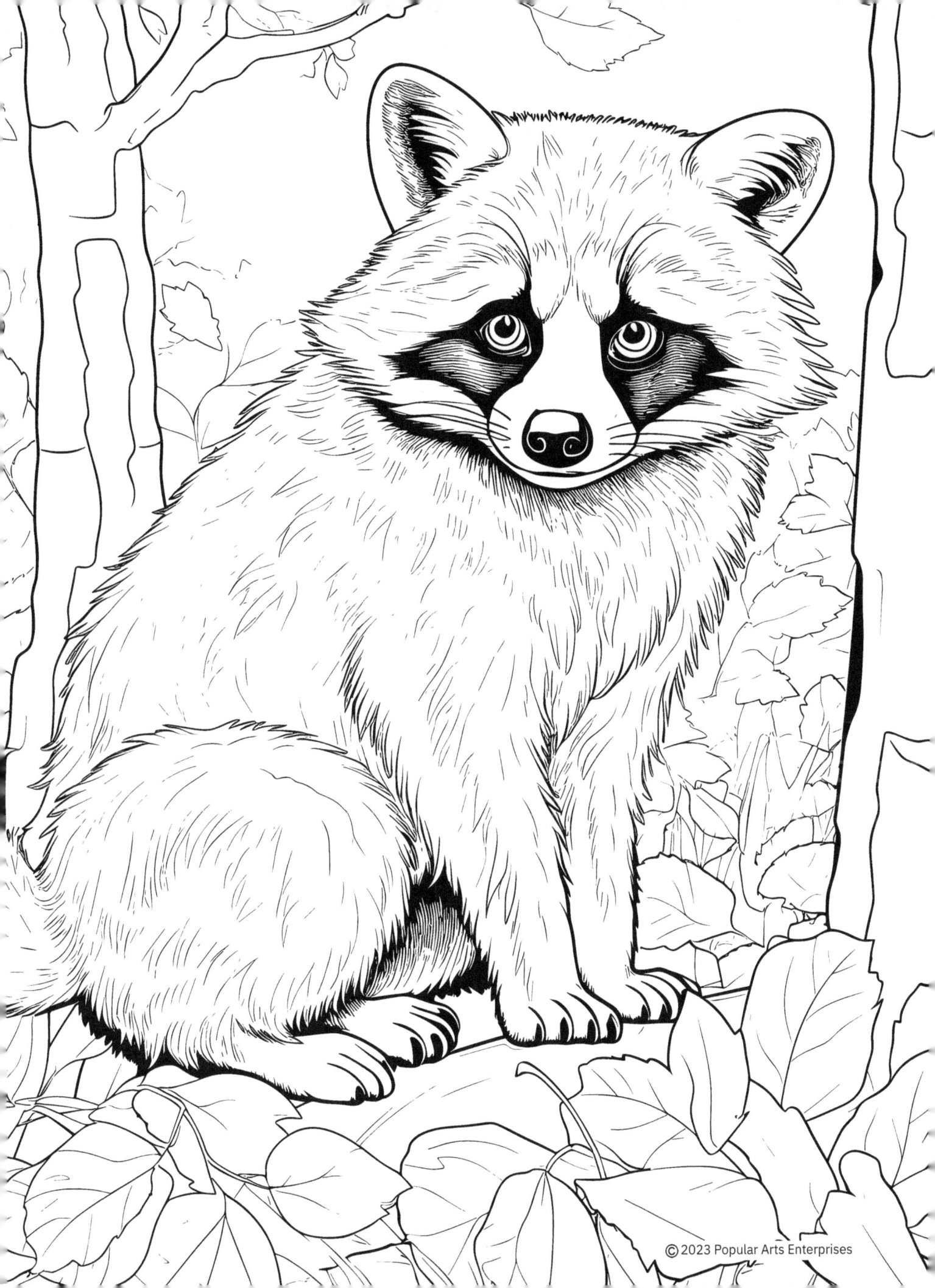

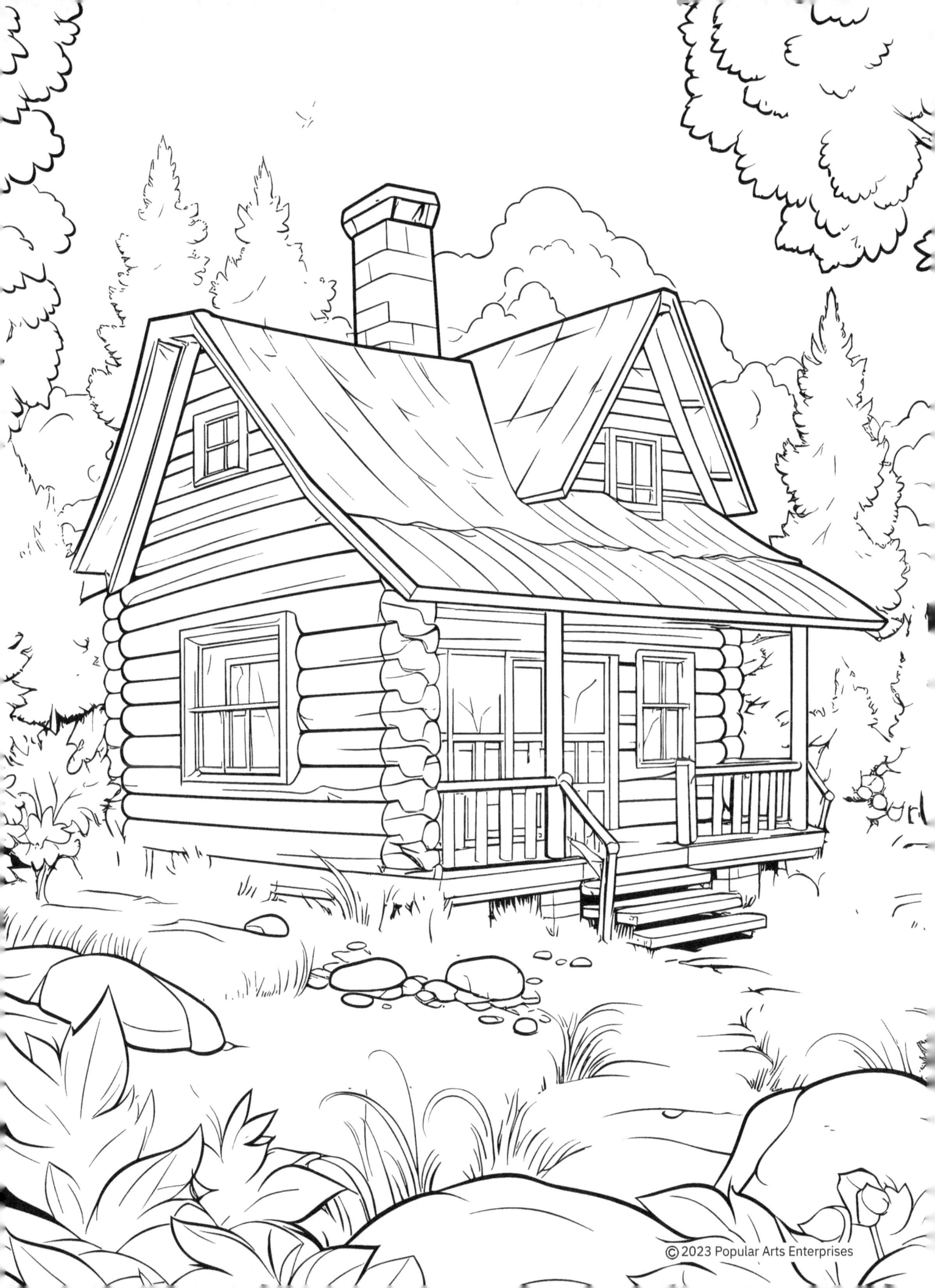

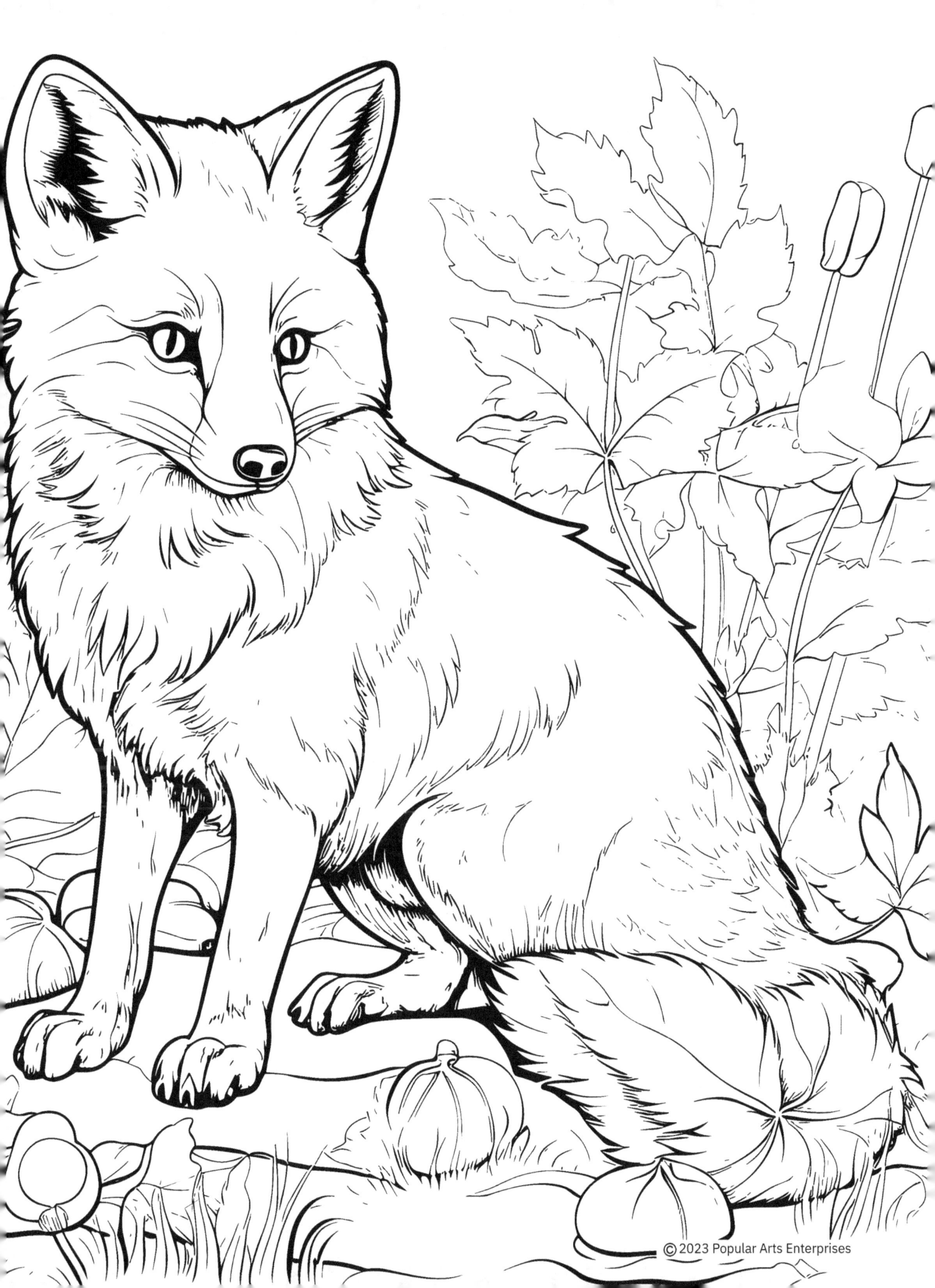

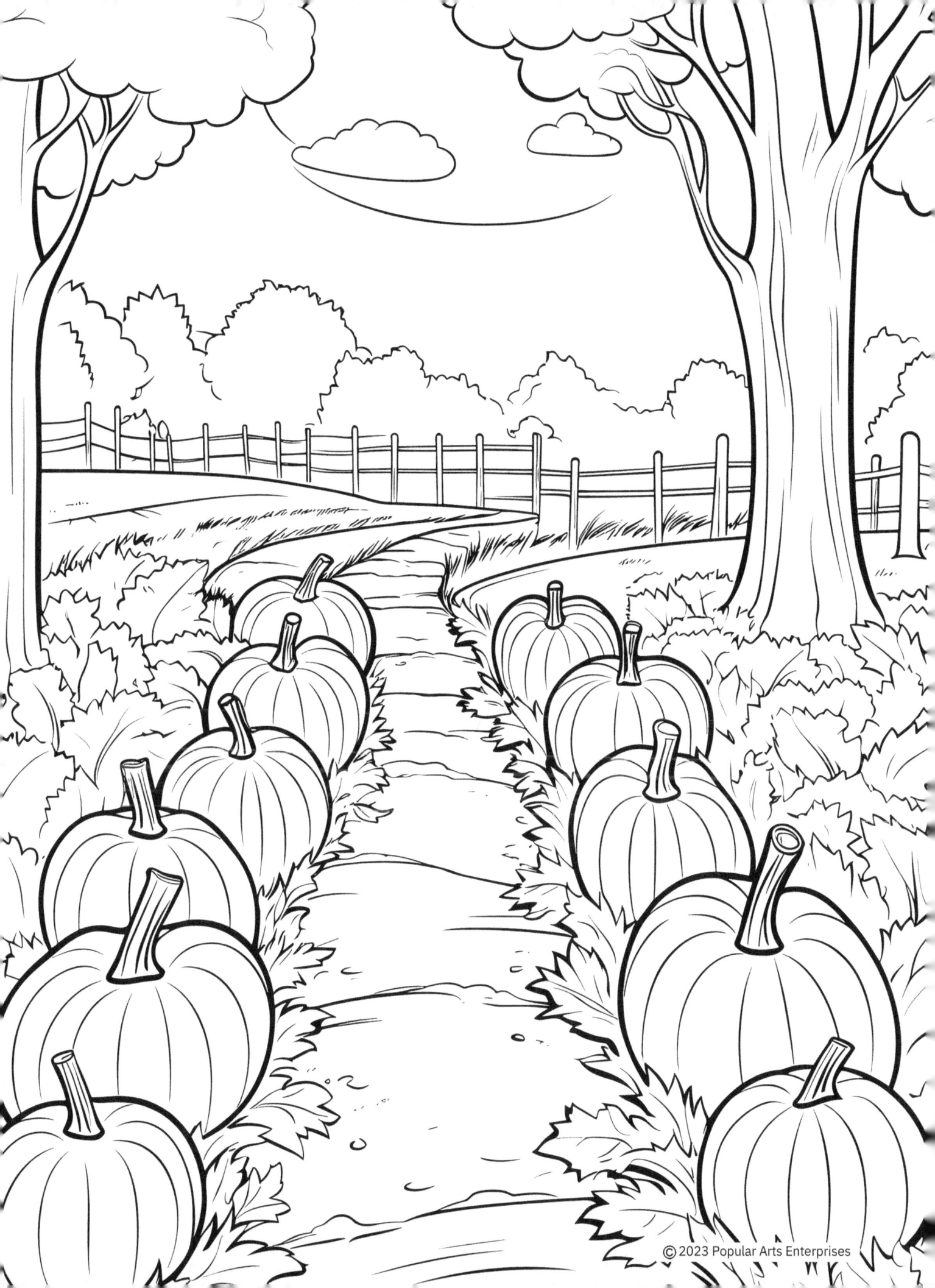

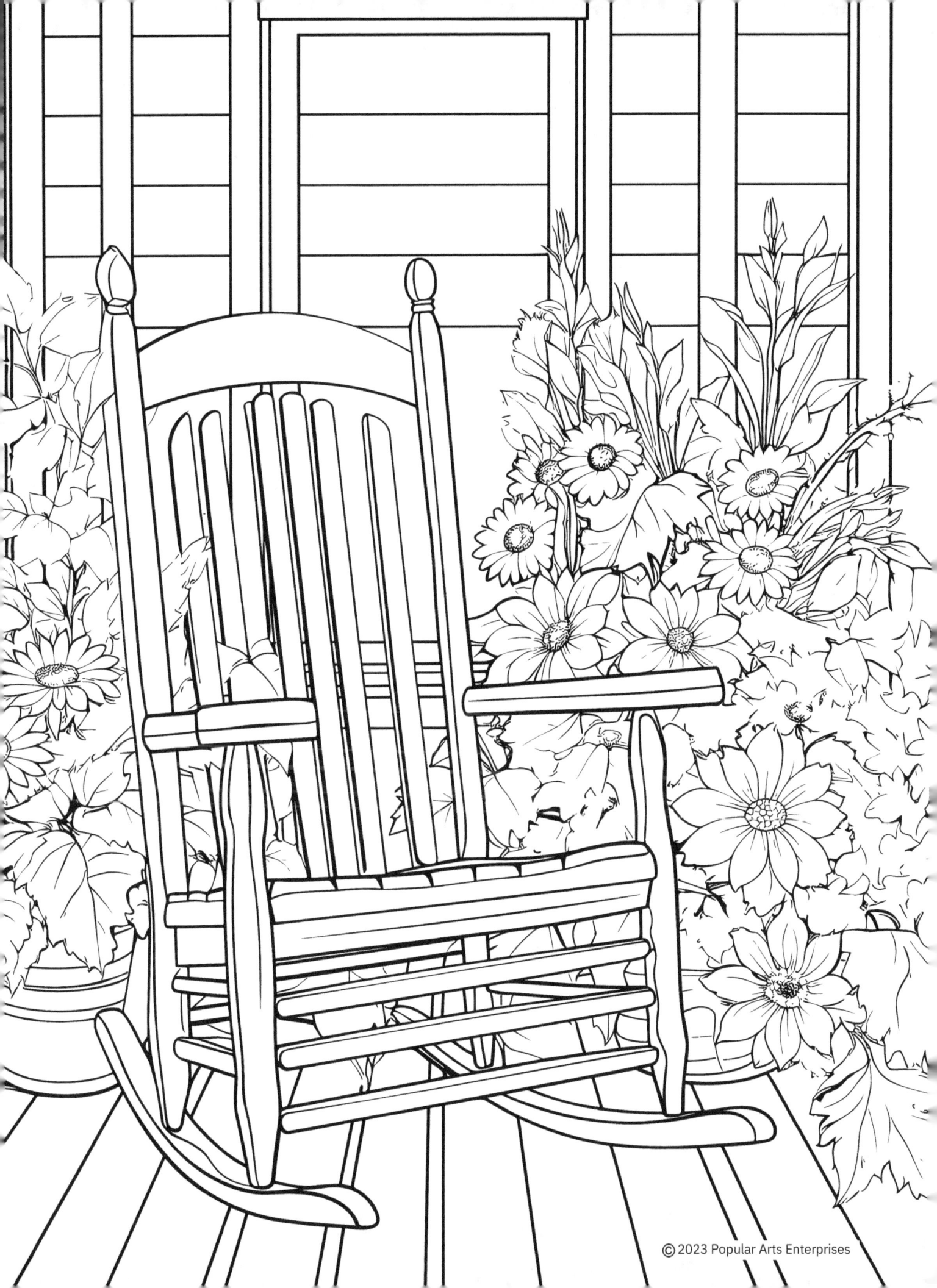

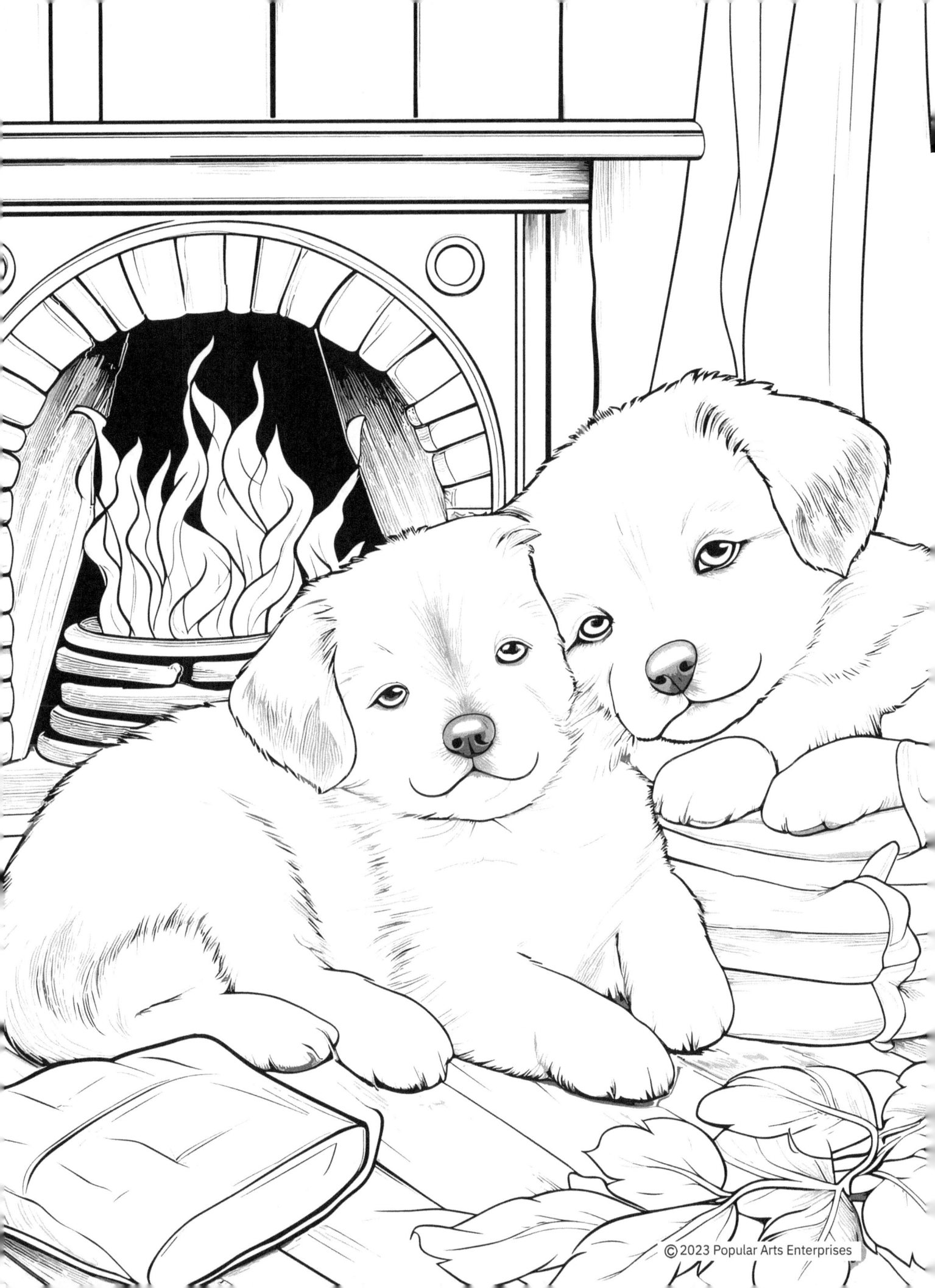

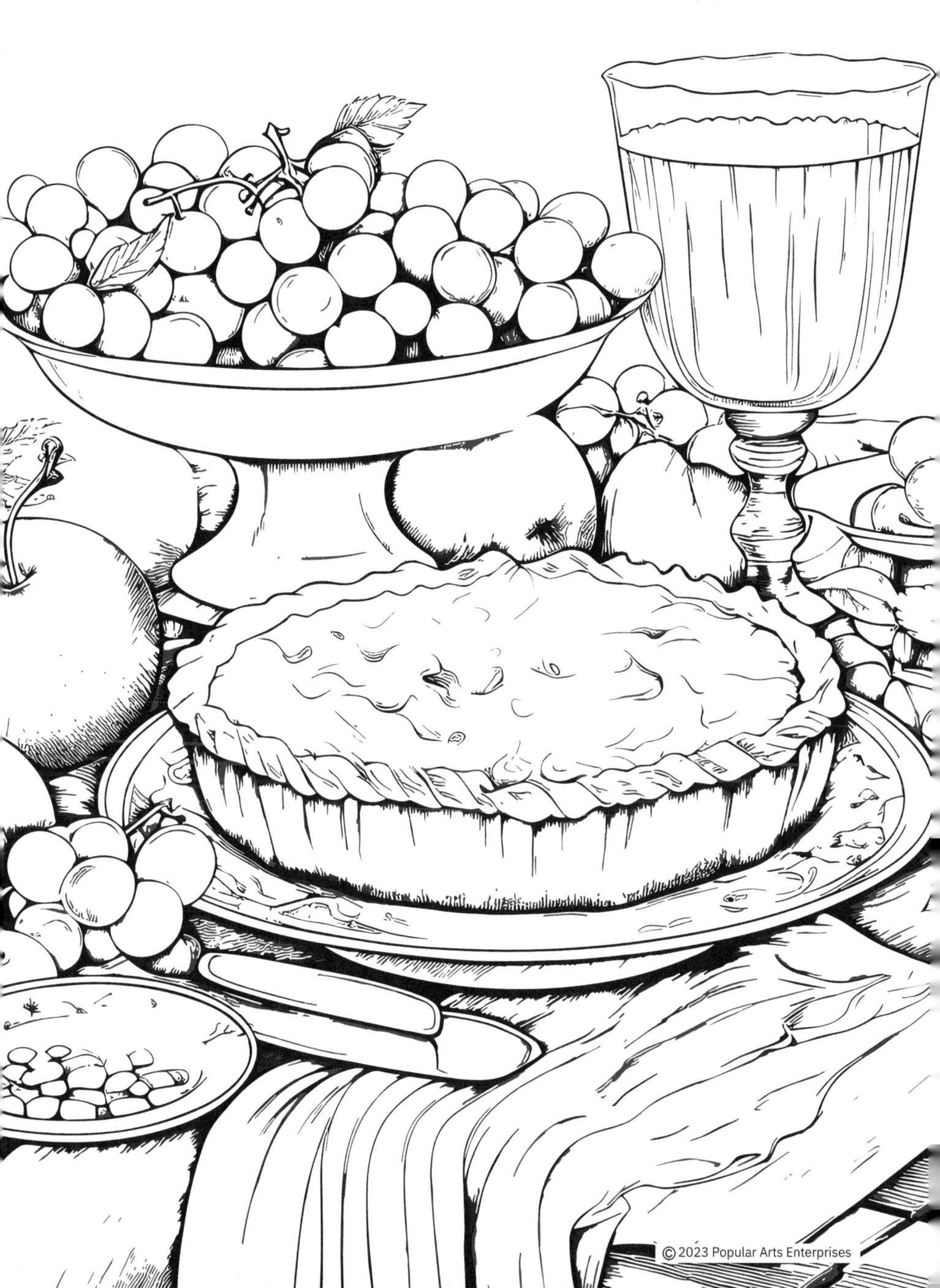

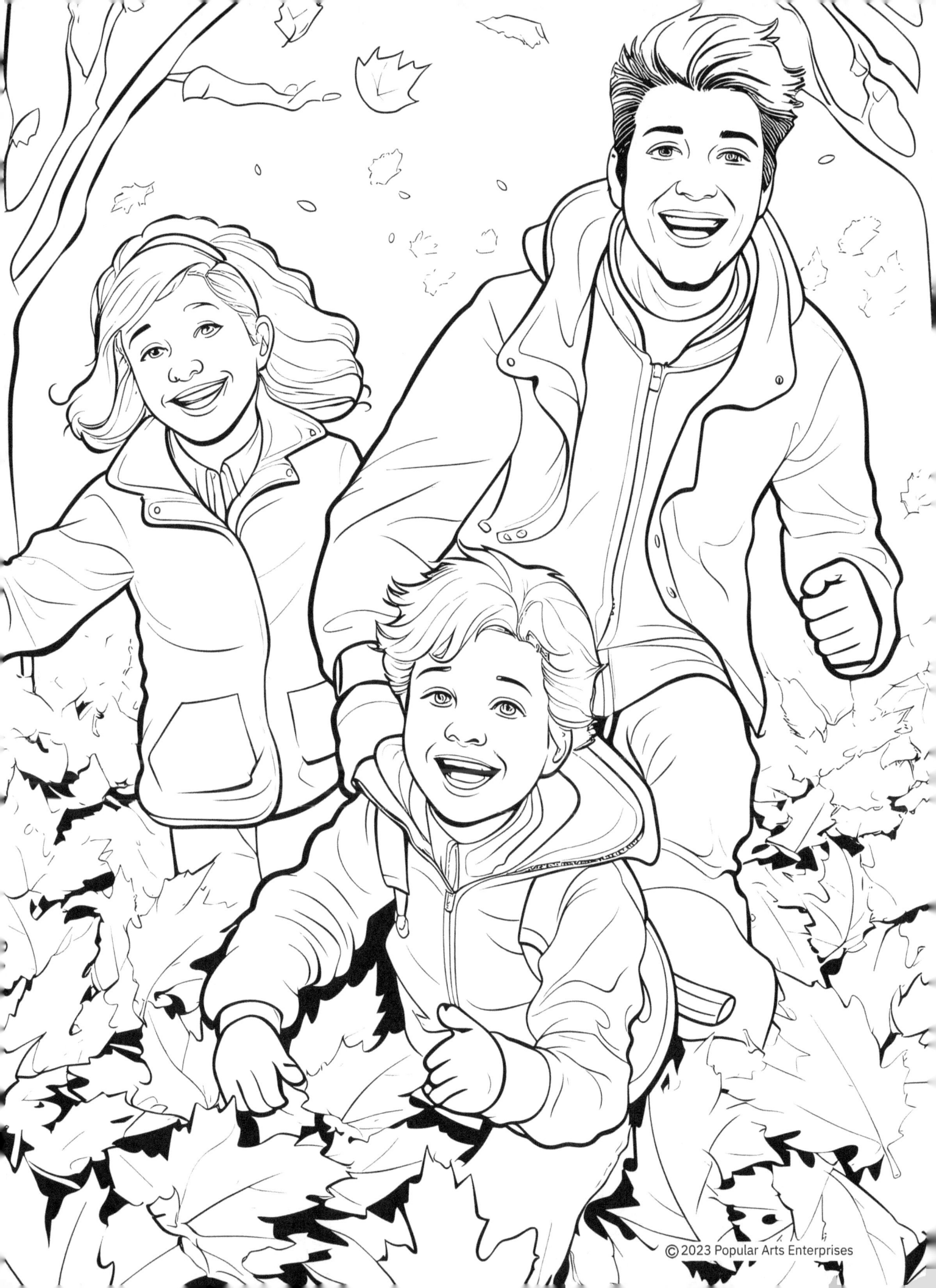

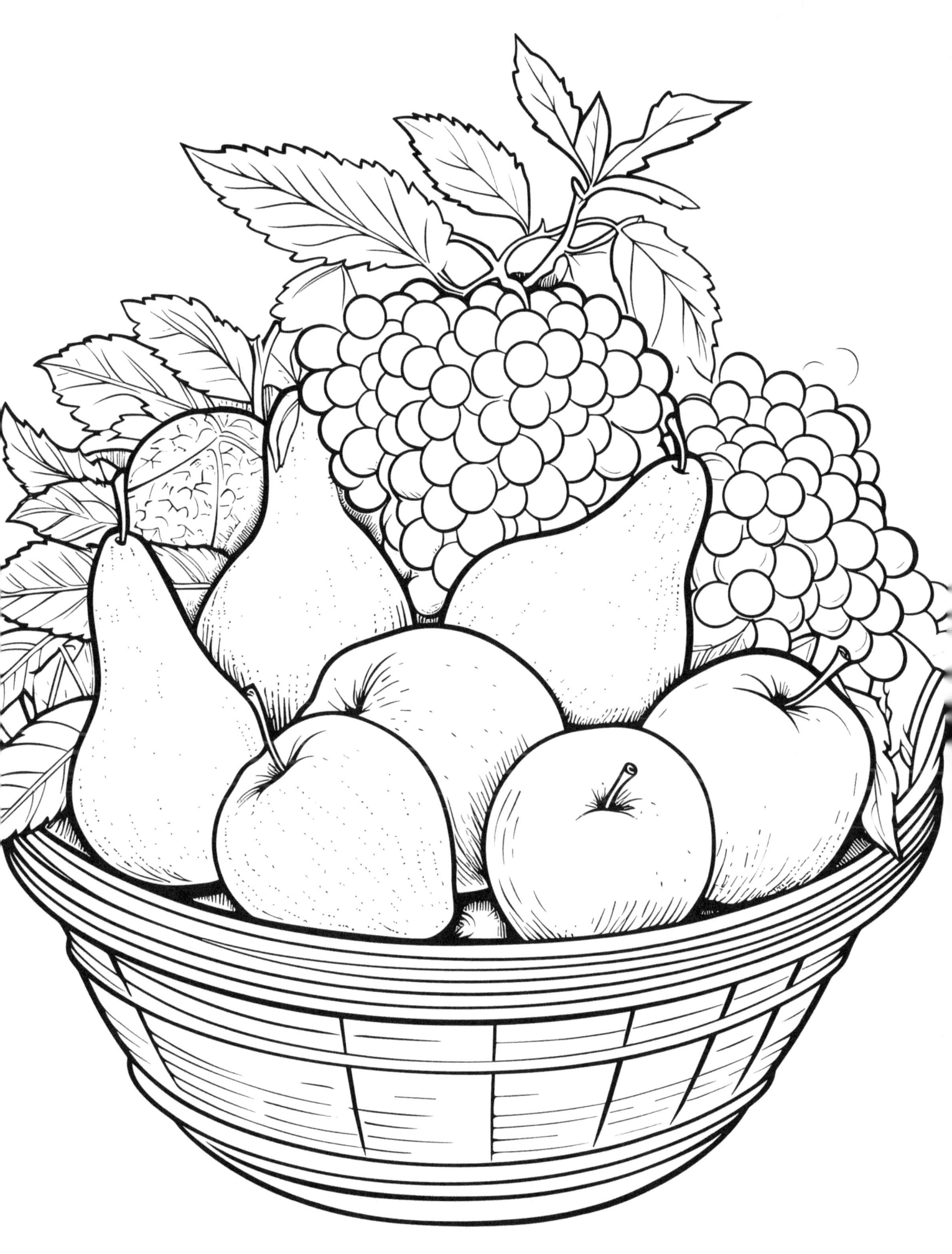

Thank You!

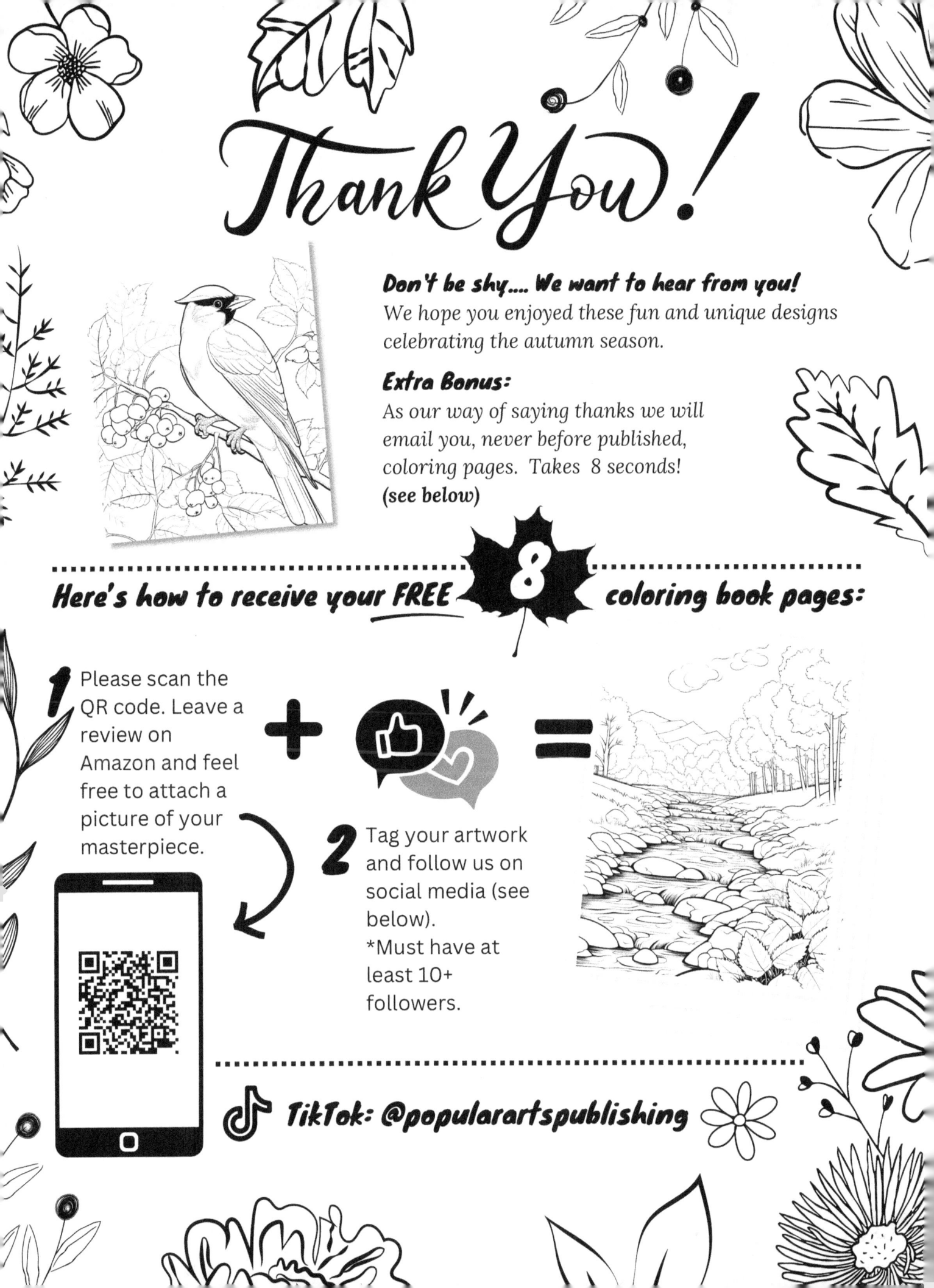

Don't be shy.... We want to hear from you!
We hope you enjoyed these fun and unique designs celebrating the autumn season.

Extra Bonus:
As our way of saying thanks we will email you, never before published, coloring pages. Takes 8 seconds!
(see below)

Here's how to receive your FREE **8** coloring book pages:

1 Please scan the QR code. Leave a review on Amazon and feel free to attach a picture of your masterpiece.

+

2 Tag your artwork and follow us on social media (see below).
*Must have at least 10+ followers.

=

TikTok: @populararartspublishing